# HIGHLIGHTS OF RECENT AMERICAN ARCHITECTURE

## A Guide to Contemporary Architects and Their Leading Works Completed 1945-1978

by

SYLVIA HART WRIGHT

The Scarecrow Press, Inc.
Metuchen, N.J., & London
1982

**Library of Congress Cataloging in Publication Data**

Wright, Sylvia Hart.
    Highlights of recent American architecture.

    Includes indexes.
    1. Architecture--United States.  2. Architecture,
Modern--20th century--United States.  3. Architects
--United States--Registers.  I. Title.
NA712.W74        720'.973          82-3391
ISBN 0-8108-1540-0               AACR2

# TABLE OF CONTENTS

ACKNOWLEDGMENTS

_____

It is a pleasure to acknowledge the help of the many people and institutions whose contributions have made this book possible.

I am deeply grateful both to The City College, City University of New York, for granting me the one-year fellowship leave during which I did most of the preliminary work for this book and to the City University's Research Foundation for granting me the PSC-CUNY Research Award which enabled me to employ a research assistant. As a scholar who is still learning in the field of architectural history, I must also acknowledge my enormous debt to the Avery Library, Columbia University, not only for its glorious collection but also for its tranquil ambience and its unfailingly gracious and cooperative staff. During my fellowship leave I virtually took up part-time residence there.

On my own campus when this project was still in the planning stages, I received valuable encouragement and advice from my then dean at the School of Architecture and Environmental Studies, Bernard P. Spring. Time and again because he was kind enough to phone on my behalf, doors opened for me to experts and resources around the country. Through his good offices I was able to meet with Richard Freeman and Susan Holton Cosgrove of the American Institute of Architects and Jeanne Butler Hodges of the AIA Foundation, each of whom contributed expertise to my budding project. Similarly, Dean Spring helped me obtain copies of rare publications concerning architectural awards from the American Institute of Steel Construction. At the AISC, Leslie H. Gillette and Helen Bronski were my obliging contacts.

Professor Virginia Cesario, Chief Librarian at City College at that time, gave me precious support and encouragement. I am indebted to her for her confidence in me and for the effort she made to assure my fellowship leave. My heartfelt thanks go also to my colleague in the Library Department, Dr. Elizabeth Rajec, for her enthusiastic and knowledgeable guidance at many stages of my research.

Looking back on this project's early stages, it is exhilarating to recall one snowy evening in Washington, D.C. when John Fondersmith, edi-

v

tor of <u>American Urban Guidenotes,</u> shared with me his encyclopedic knowledge and his devotion to architectural lore. Soon thereafter, Elliot Willensky also gave me useful advice. As my research progressed, Professors Paul David Pearson and Norval White of the City College School of Architecture were kind enough to give me the benefit of their experience as authors, architects and architectural scholars.

Prof. Robert Kuhner of the City College Library made several useful suggestions about the format and contents of this study. Catha Grace Rambusch of the Committee for the Preservation of Architectural Records amiably offered constructive comments and alerted me to significant developments in the field. It was she who put me in touch with Prof. Carol Krinsky, New York University, who obligingly supplied detailed data regarding the Albany Mall. It was also my great good fortune, as I labored away at Avery Library, to elicit the attention and help of the incomparable Adolf Placzek. My conversations with him were a never failing source of clarification and reassurance. I shall always be grateful to him not only for his wisdom but for his unfailing courtesy and grace in initiating a relative novice into the intricacies of planning and completing a study of this sort.

My colleagues in the Association of Architecture School Librarians contributed to this work in many ways. Special thanks are due to Elaine Arnold, Imre Meszaros, and Doris Wheeler who supplied hard-to-find information about buildings in their localities and to Mary Dunnigan, Maryellen Lo Presti and Jane McMaster who supplied other forms of professional assistance. More staff members than I can name at architectural firms, corporate offices, and cultural institutions around the country gave generously of their time and resources to confirm building completion dates and other data and to send the deluge of handsome photographs from which this volume's illustrations were selected. Fran Gretes of Skidmore, Owings & Merrill and Serena Rattazi of the Albright-Knox Art Gallery were particularly helpful.

The wit and intellectual insight of Susan Kaplan, my first research assistant, brightened the early days of this project. Marie-Alice Souffrant, my research assistant in its latter days, eased immeasurably the chores of compiling the indexes and preparing the final manuscript with her quiet charm, her unfailing patience and her determined commitment to accuracy.

As this project neared completion, Profs. Robert Alan Cordingley and Norval White here at City College made room in their busy schedules to read the manuscript, suggesting ways to refine it. Though it was my pleasure to avail myself of their skilled guidance, the responsibility for whatever shortcomings may remain, of course, must rest entirely with me.

Finally, with gratitude, love and something of chagrin, I must note here the massive contribution made to this effort by my husband, Paul Fletcher, and our son, Rustin. For over two years, they have cheered me up when I grumbled about my self-imposed overload and have jauntily fended for themselves when I neglected housewifery for scholarly pursuits. Without their forbearance this book never would have come to be.

# PREFACE

This volume is a guide to basic information about 379 of the most widely reviewed American buildings and complexes completed from 1945 through 1978. Architects, whatever their nationality, are represented here if they have designed especially noted buildings erected in the United States, Canada or Puerto Rico.

Types of structures vary widely: they range from trend-setting office buildings like Equitable Savings and Loan in Oregon and Lever House in New York to the solar telescope at Kitt Peak, Arizona and rapid transit stations in Chicago and Washington, D.C. Here are prizewinning laboratories and factories, theaters and schools, apartment houses, churches and multi-use complexes. Some outstanding examples of adaptive re-use, such as Ghirardelli Square in San Francisco and Boston's Faneuil Hall, have been included. However, no attempt has been made to cover either individual residences (which alone could fill several volumes this size) or open space developments such as plazas and malls unless they incorporate buildings as well.

The arrangement of data in this book is designed to help solve one of the most vexing and pervasive problems of research in the field of architecture. Most indexing of magazines and cataloging of books assume that the researcher already knows the name of the architect whose building is to be studied. Yet, in reality, students and architecture buffs frequently plunge into a search knowing little more than the names and locations of the buildings that interest them--and they may not be sure of those. Unless they have entree to a very extensive architectural library and a knowledgeable librarian, they are likely to find their efforts stymied from the start.

The main body of this guide is arranged alphabetically by architect's surname; however, a series of indexes keyed to entry numbers in the main listing has been provided to allow access to information about notable examples of contemporary architecture by many other routes. Thus, the reader can look up a building under its name or variant names, under its geographical location and--for good measure--under its building type.

The Building Type Index runs from "Airports" to "Zoo Buildings" and includes 43 subject headings and numerous cross-references. Nearly half the buildings covered in this book appear under more than one heading in this index.[1] It can be used to identify the most noted contemporary exemplars of such varied architectural forms as concert halls and jails, sports facilities and condominiums, planetariums, winter gardens, and planned communities. Architecture students working on design projects should find it a useful starting point for their research and it is hoped that architects, too, will find it of interest.

The main entry about each building provides a summary of salient facts about it. These include its location, the date of its completion,[2] a brief description usually based on reviews published soon after its completion, major honors it has received,[3] a citation to one or more articles about it,[4] and (to the extent such information is available and space permits) the names of professionals and firms significantly involved in its design and construction, e.g., associated architects, engineers, and landscape architects. Since the names of these professionals and firms are included in a fourth and final index, this volume also may be used as a convenient reference source for career information about them. Meanwhile, occasional annotations inserted in the main body of the text record such miscellaneous addenda as the gold medals won by leading architects.

As suggested above, the author has sought to include the period's most noted buildings, that is, those which have been written about most extensively. The great majority of the 379 buildings and complexes covered here have received the acclaim of architects, architectural historians, and other experts in the field. It is hoped that most of the great architectural achievements of the post-World War II era in America are listed here. However, inclusion has not been limited to these uncontested successes. Here also are buildings and complexes that have attracted attention primarily as the biggest, the most conspicuous or the most controversial. Thus, flipping through these pages you may run across the Watergate Apartments and the Albany Mall, the Pan Am Building and Pruitt-Igoe, the Lyndon Baines Johnson Library, Disneyland and Simon Rodilla's fantastic towers in Watts.

In selecting buildings for inclusion in this book, the author has tried to avoid subjective judgments. With advice and assistance from experts in the fields of architecture, architectural history, and librarianship, a system of objective criteria was devised whereby points were awarded for each honor a building won, each major reference to it in a respected book and each article about it in an architectural magazine. No doubt, despite this screening process and the author's best efforts, some worthy subjects have been overlooked while others less worthy have been included. For such regrettable but perhaps inevitable shortcomings, the author offers sincere apologies. It is hoped that at some future date such oversights may be corrected in a revised edition.

S. H. W.

1. To cite a few examples: the Beinecke Rare Book and Manuscript Library at Yale appears under both "Libraries" and "Universities and Colleges--Buildings and Campuses"; Westbeth Artists Housing in New York is listed under both "Housing" and "Restoration, Renovation and Adaptive Re-Use"; the Hennepin County Government Center in Minneapolis, whose twin towers are designed for disparate uses, can be found under "Courthouses," "Office Buildings," and "State Capitols, City Halls and Civic Centers."

   Cross-references are designed to guide the reader to appropriate headings; e.g., for both "County Office Complexes" and "Municipal Office Complexes," the reader is referred to "State Capitols, City Halls and Civic Centers."

2. No attempt has been made to supply starting dates. Dates of completion have been taken, wherever possible, from the most reliable contemporary sources. Where inconsistencies in the literature could not be resolved, alternate dates may be shown with a slash between them, e.g. "1968/1970." Since the "completion" of a building may be dated from the completion of its final drawings, the issuance of its occupancy certificate or the occasion of its dedication, and since inevitably some buildings are refined after their official opening, more than one completion date may be arguable.

3. Numerous cultural groups, industrial institutes and professional associations, both local and national, grant architectural awards. The limited scope of this study permitted inclusion of only the most widely publicized of these. For a list of all honors systematically cited, see the section, "User's Guide."

4. Bibliographic references are selective, not comprehensive. Whenever possible, references are given to relatively long, well illustrated articles in widely distributed--i.e., readily available--journals or books, preferably in English. If no single article on a given building fits that description, several shorter, less complete articles or books with relevant segments may be cited. Similarly, if a building has elicited widely differing opinions, contrasting articles may be cited. The goal throughout has been to supply reliable information on the completed building. Articles published well before the building's completion generally are not cited.

USER'S GUIDE

---

In headings for the Guide to Contemporary Architects and Their Leading Works, the names of individual architects are never inverted, though they are arranged alphabetically by surname. Joint ventures are indicated by two or more firm names listed with semicolons between, with cross-references provided from latter firms to the primary name.

The first sentence of each entry supplies basic information in the following order: Building Name; Location; Date of Completion.

In accordance with the scheme recommended by the United States Postal Service, the fifty states, the District of Columbia and the Commonwealth of Puerto Rico are abbreviated as follows:

| | | | |
|---|---|---|---|
| AK | Alaska | ME | Maine |
| AL | Alabama | MI | Michigan |
| AR | Arkansas | MN | Minnesota |
| AZ | Arizona | MO | Missouri |
| CA | California | MS | Mississippi |
| CO | Colorado | MT | Montana |
| CT | Connecticut | NC | North Carolina |
| DC | District of Columbia | ND | North Dakota |
| DE | Delaware | NE | Nebraska |
| FL | Florida | NH | New Hampshire |
| GA | Georgia | NJ | New Jersey |
| HI | Hawaii | NM | New Mexico |
| IA | Iowa | NV | Nevada |
| ID | Idaho | NY | New York |
| IL | Illinois | OH | Ohio |
| IN | Indiana | OK | Oklahoma |
| KS | Kansas | OR | Oregon |
| KY | Kentucky | PA | Pennsylvania |
| LA | Louisiana | PR | Puerto Rico |
| MA | Massachusetts | RI | Rhode Island |
| MD | Maryland | SC | South Carolina |

| SD | South Dakota | VT | Vermont |
|----|--------------|----|---------|
| TN | Tennessee | WA | Washington |
| TX | Texas | WI | Wisconsin |
| UT | Utah | WV | West Virginia |
| VA | Virginia | WY | Wyoming |

The following list provides explanations of abbreviations and awards cited within entries in the guide:

AIA--The American Institute of Architects.

AIA ARCHITECTURAL FIRM AWARD--This award is given by the American Institute of Architects to "a firm which has consistently produced distinguished architecture for a period of at least ten years."

AIA BICENTENNIAL LIST--The July 1976 issue of the AIA Journal contains a section entitled "Highlights of American Architecture, 1776-1976." Here are summarized the responses of 46 architectural "practitioners, historians and critics" who had been asked "to nominate up to 29 of what they considered the proudest achievements of American architecture over the past 200 years."

AIA HONOR AND MERIT AWARDS--In 1949, the American Institute of Architects initiated the practice of annually conferring both Honor Awards and Awards of Merit on outstanding architectural achievements, many but not all of which had been completed within the previous year. In 1967, the Awards of Merit category was discontinued.

AIA TWENTY-FIVE YEAR AWARD--Each year since 1969, with the exception of 1970, the American Institute of Architects has selected one 25- to 35-year-old project to receive this award "given in recognition of architectural design of enduring significance."

AISC--The American Institute of Steel Construction. Since 1960, the AISC annually has conferred several Architectural Awards of Excellence on buildings in which steel has been used with particular distinction.

BARD AWARD--Since 1964, with the exception of 1974, the City Club of New York annually has conferred the Albert S. Bard Award for Excellence in Architecture and Urban Design on outstanding examples of architectural achievement in New York.

BARTLETT AWARD--Named for the late Senator E. L. Bartlett of Alaska, author of Public Law 90-480 on barrier-free design, this award is bestowed annually by the American Institute of Architects on those AIA Honor Award winners which are judged to be most accessible to the handicapped and the elderly. It has been granted since 1969.

KEMPER AWARD--The Edward C. Kemper Award is given each year by the American Institute of Architects to "one AIA member who has contributed significantly to the Institute and to the profession."

PA--<u>Progressive Architecture</u>, one of the leading architecture magazines in the United States. Since 1954 it has conferred Design Citations, Award Citations and Design Awards on distinguished architectural projects, announcing winners regularly in its January issues. Unlike the other honors listed here, <u>PA</u>'s awards are conferred for designs that at the time have not yet been built.

R. S. REYNOLDS MEMORIAL AWARD--This award, sponsored by Reynolds Metal Company, is administered by the American Institute of Architects. Each year it honors one "permanent, significant work of architecture, in the creation of which aluminum has been an important contributing factor."

RIBA--Royal Institute of British Architects.

RIBA JOURNAL--The journal of the Royal Institute of British Architects.

ROYAL GOLD MEDAL--Since 1848, the British sovereign each year has conferred one Royal Gold Medal for the promotion of Architecture "on some distinguished architect, or group of architects for work of high merit, or on some distinguished person or group whose work has promoted ... the advancement of Architecture."

HIGHLIGHTS

OF

RECENT

AMERICAN

ARCHITECTURE

# GUIDE TO CONTEMPORARY ARCHITECTS AND
# THEIR LEADING WORKS

---

## ALVAR AALTO
Winner of Royal Gold Medal, 1957, and AIA Gold Metal, 1963.

---

1. Baker House, Massachusetts Institute of Technology; Cambridge, MA; 1948. Built as a senior dorm and including a large dining hall, it winds, serpentine fashion, along the banks of the Charles River and is accented by a huge "V" of outdoor staircases hung dramatically against one long side. Associated architects: Perry, Shaw & Hepburn. Contractor: Aberthaw Co. SEE: Architectural Forum (vol. 91) August 1949, 61-69.

2. Mount Angel Abbey Library; St. Benedict, OR; 1970. This library for a Benedictine monastery fans out over its site on a wooded knoll. Inside, it features a three-story-high reading and stack area enhanced by a curving skylight overhead. Designer in charge for Alvar Aalto: Erik T. Variainen; executive architects: DeMars & Wells. Structural engineer: S. J. Medwadowski. Acoustical consultant: Walter Soroka. Contractor: Reimers & Jolivette. SEE: Architectural Record (vol. 149) May 1971, 111-116. Alvar Aalto. (Architectural Monographs no. 4.) New York: Rizzoli, 1979.

---

## MAX ABRAMOVITZ

---

3. Avery Fisher Hall, Lincoln Center; New York, NY; 1962--interior frequently reconstructed thereafter. Originally designed to seat 2644 and to be the permanent home of the Philharmonic orchestra, this concert hall--originally known as Philharmonic Hall--proved to have

such disappointing acoustics that its interior, housed within a travertine and glass facade, was repeatedly modified. In 1976, it was completely gutted and rebuilt with what appeared to be satisfactory results. For original structure: Engineers: Ammann & Whitney (structural); Syska & Hennessy (mechanical/electrical). Acoustical consultants: Bolt, Beranek & Newman. For interior reconstruction, 1976: architects: Philip Johnson and John Burgee. Consultants: Cyril Harris (acoustical); Ammann & Whitney (structural); Syska & Hennessy (mechanical). SEE: Architectural Record (vol. 132) September 1962, 136-139. Progressive Architecture (vol. 58) March 1977, 64-69.

---

## AFFLECK, DESBARATS, DIMAKOPOULOS, LEBENSOLD, SISE

---

4. Place Bonaventure; Montreal, Quebec, Canada; 1967. A multi-use complex which has been called "an underground city," it comprises such varied facilities as shopping arcades, office space, a large hotel and an exhibition hall--all served by a 1000-car garage and a weather protected pedestrian network. Partner in charge: R. T. Affleck. Structural consultants: R. R. Nicolet & Associates; Lalonde, Valois, Lamarre, Valois & Associates. Mechanical and electrical consultants: James P. Keith & Associates. Contractor: Concordia Estates Ltd. SEE: Architecture Canada: The RAIC Journal (vol. 44) July 1967, 31-39.

---

## LAWRENCE B. ANDERSON, supervising architect

---

5. Suburban campus, Rochester Institute of Technology; near Rochester, NY; 1968. When this privately supported technical school decided to move to a one-mile-square suburban site, design responsibilities were shared by landscape architect Dan Kiley and five architects--Edward Larrabee Barnes, Kevin Roche and John Dinkeloo, Hugh Stubbins, and Harry M. Weese--cooperating under the supervision of Lawrence B. Anderson of Anderson, Beckwith and Haible. Exteriors throughout were faced with identical pinkish-brown brick, some 7,000,000 bricks in all. HONORS: New York State/AIA Award for Community Design. SEE: Architectural Record (vol. 144) November 1968, 123-[134].

---

## JOHN ANDREWS

---

6. George Gund Hall, Harvard U.; Cambridge, MA; 1972. Houses all

programs and facilities of the Graduate School of Design and features a grandly spacious central studio shared by architects, planners, urban designers and others. Designers: John Andrews, Edward R. Baldwin and John Simpson; partner in charge: Edward R. Baldwin. Engineers: LeMessurier Assoc. (structural); G. Granek & Associates (mechanical). Landscape architects: Richard Strong Associates. HONORS: AIA Honor Award, 1973; Bartlett Award, 1973. SEE: Architectural Record (vol. 152) November 1972, 95-104.

7. Scarborough College, U. of Toronto; Scarborough, Ontario, Canada; 1966. This blocky, angular megastructure comprises science and humanities wings, an administrative area and a refectory. Associated architects: Page & Steele; planner: Michael Hugo-Brunt; landscape architect: Michael Hough & Associates. Engineering consultants: Ewbank Pillar & Associates. SEE: Architectural Forum (vol. 124) May 1966, 30-[41], [52]-[55].

## ANSHEN & ALLEN

8. Chapel of the Holy Cross; Sedona, AZ; 1956 (Illus. 1). A Roman Catholic chapel in a rugged mountain setting, designed to seat 50-150 worshippers. The great cross centered in its SW wall soars upward 90 feet from its base framed between massive boulders. Engineers: Robert D. Dewell (civil/structural); Earl & Gropp (electrical/mechanical). Sculptor of Corpus over altar: Keith Monroe. HONORS: PA Award Citation, 1954; AIA Honor Award, 1957. SEE: Architectural Record (vol. 120) October 1956, 173-182.

## THE ARCHITECTS COLLABORATIVE (TAC)
Winner, the AIA's Architectural Firm Award, 1964. This firm's senior and most famous member, Walter Gropius, 1883-1969, won Great Britain's Royal Gold Medal in 1956 and the AIA Gold Medal in 1959. Other TAC members have included Jean Bodman Fletcher, Norman Fletcher, John C. Harkness, Sarah Harkness, Robert S. McMillan, Louis A. McMillen and Benjamin Thompson. SEE ALSO: separate listing for Benjamin Thompson, practicing independently.

9. American Institute of Architects National Headquarters Building; Washington, DC; 1973. In 1963, Mitchell/Giurgola Associates won a competition to design AIA headquarters; however, they met with a series of adverse rulings from the city's Fine Arts Commission. Ultimately, TAC's design was adopted instead. A low, modern office building, it curves gracefully around its historic neighbor, the Octagon, built in

1. Chapel of the Holy Cross.    Anshen & Allen.
   Photo:  Julius Shulman

1800 and occupied briefly by Pres. Madison. Principal in charge:
Norman C. Fletcher. Landscape designers: Knox C. Johnson,
Hugh T. Kirkley. Engineers: LeMessurier Associates (structural);
Cosentini Associates (mechanical). SEE: AIA Journal (vol. 59)
June 1973, 19-56. Architectural Record (vol. 153) May 1973, 131-
140.

10. C. Thurston Chase Learning Center, Eaglebrook School; Deerfield, MA;
1966. A cluster of three low-slung, understated buildings houses
classrooms, a language lab, a science wing, a meeting hall and an
inviting, airy library. Associated architects: Campbell, Aldrich &
Nulty. Structural engineers: Souza & True. HONORS: AIA Honor
Award, 1967; AISC Architectural Award of Excellence, 1968. SEE:
Architectural Record (vol. 139) Feb. 1966, 163-182.

11. Children's Hospital Medical Center; Boston, MA; 1970. To accommodate a growing medical center, TAC created a tall residential tower
to house hospital staff flanked by a low, street-oriented "Children's
Inn" for ambulatory patients accompanied by parents. Principals in
charge: John C. Harkness, Roland Kluver, Jean Fletcher. Engineers: Souza & True (structural); Metcalf & Eddy and Francis Associates (mechanical). Landscape architect: Laurence Zuelke.
General contractor: Turner Construction Co. HONORS: AIA Honor
Award, 1971. SEE: Architectural Record (vol. 140) October 1966,
204-205. Baumeister (vol. 67) September 1970, 1018-1021. AIA
Journal (vol. 55) June 1971, 45-55.

12. Harvard University Graduate Center; Cambridge, MA; 1950. Aiming
for "the illusion of motion," the Center's eight buildings--most of
them linked by covered walks--enclose a series of quadrangles.
Seven of the eight are dormitories; the eighth, the Commons, provides dining rooms, lounges, and space for large meetings. Job
captain: Walter Gropius. For Commons Building: Norman Fletcher;
for dorms: Robert McMillan; site improvements: Louis McMillen.
Technical associates: Brown, Lawford & Forbes. Engineers: Mau-
rice A. Reidy (structural); Charles T. Main (mechanical). Contractors: George A. Fuller & Co. HONORS: AIA Bicentennial List,
1 nomination. SEE: Architectural Forum (vol. 93) December 1950,
62-71.

13. Johns-Manville World Headquarters; near Denver, CO; 1976 (Illus. 2).
Deftly engineered and sleekly sheathed in aluminum, this corporate
headquarters spans a wide reach of foothills and looks out over a
desert valley. Principals in charge: William Geddis, Joseph D.
Hoskins; project architects for design: John P. Sheehy and Michael
Gebhart. Landscape: Robert DeWolfe and David Mittelstadt. Consultants: LeMessurier Associates, SCI (structural); Golder, Fass
Assoc. (foundations); Cosentini Associates (mechanical/electrical/
acoustical). Construction manager: Turner Construction Co.
HONORS: AIA Bicentennial List - 1 nomination. SEE: Architectural Record (vol. 162) September 1977, 89-100.

2. Johns-Manville World Headquarters. The Architects Collaborative.
   Photo: © Nick Wheeler

14. Social Science Center (1961) and Academic Quadrangle (1962), Brandeis
    University; Waltham, MA. Both of these campus clusters are built
    of reinforced concrete enlivened by meticulous attention to detail.
    Edges and corners are rounded, a carefully selected range of colors
    in the aggregate is brought out by bushhammering, and rosy brick
    walls lend contrast inside and out. Partner in charge: Benjamin
    Thompson. Engineers: Simpson, Gumpertz and Heger (structural,
    for Social Science Center), Goldberg LeMessurier & Associates
    (structural, for Academic Quadrangle); Reardon & Turner (mechan-
    ical). Contractor: G. B. H. Macomber Co. HONORS: AIA
    Merit Award, 1963, for Academic Quadrangle. SEE: Architectural
    Record (vol. 116) Jan. 1962, [121]-[126]. Architectural Design
    (vol. 32) April 1962, 194-197.

## ARCHITECTURAL ASSOCIATES COLORADO

15. Engineering Science Center, U. of Colorado; Boulder, CO; 1965. Stone, precast concrete and concrete block combine to shape "a campus within a campus," varied environments for labs, classes, offices--and, in an unexpected courtyard, quiet reflection. Architectural Associates Colorado: William C. Muchow Assoc.; Hobart D. Wagener & Associates; Fisher & Davis. Partner in charge: William C. Muchow. Design consultants: Pietro Belluschi; and Sasaki, Dawson, DeMay Associates (site planners and landscape architects). Structural engineers: Ketchum & Konkel. HONORS: PA Design Citation, 1963. SEE: Progressive Architecture (vol. 47) November 1966, 118-131.

## WARREN H. ASHLEY

16. Edgemont Junior-Senior High School; Greenburgh, NY; 1956. Inexpensively built and energy efficient, this clean-lined, suburban educational complex makes canny use of its 70-acre site. Site planners: C. A. Currier & Associates. Engineers: Marchant & Minges. HONORS: AIA Honor Award, 1957. SEE: Architectural Record (vol. 120) September 1956, 205-209.

ASHLEY, MYER & ASSOCIATES see HUGH STUBBINS; ASHLEY, MYER & ASSOCIATES

## EDWARD LARRABEE BARNES
In 1980, his firm won the AIA's Architectural Firm Award.

17. Crown Center;* Kansas City, MO; in progress (Illus. 3). Planning for this urban renewal development sponsored by Hallmark Cards began in 1958; target date for completion is 1983. Already completed be-

*On July 17, 1981, walkways in the lobby of the Hyatt Regency Hotel here collapsed, killing over 100 and injuring many more. The Hyatt Regency was designed by a consortium of architects: Duncan Architects, Patty Berkebile Nelson Assoc., Monroe & Lefebvre; contractors: Eldridge & Son.

3. Crown Center. Edward Larrabee Barnes.
   Photo: Jim Hedrich, Hedrich-Blessing


fore 1980 were a 730-room hotel, an office complex, gardens, tennis
courts and many other amenities. Coordinating architect and master
planner: Edward Larrabee Barnes. For Crown Center Hotel, architect: Harry Weese & Associates. For Crown Center Office Complex,
architect: Edward Larrabee Barnes. Associated architects: Marshall
& Brown. Engineers: Marshall & Brown (structural); Joseph R. Loring & Associates (mechanical/electrical). Landscape consultant: Peter
C. Rolland & Associates. General contractor: Eldridge & Son. SEE:
Architectural Record (vol. 154) October 1973, [113]-[125]. Buildings (vol. 69) January 1975, 40-[46]. Process: Architecture (no.
11) 1979, 82-87.

18. State University of New York at Potsdam, overall campus plan and
    several buildings; Potsdam, NY; 1972. To pull together randomly
    placed existing buildings, Barnes designed several major additions--
    including a library, student union, dorms and lecture halls--then
    added gates to define further two major quadrangles. Three young-
    er architects--Giovanni Pasanella, Joseph G. Merz, and Richard
    Moger--were commissioned to design other campus buildings under

his supervision.    SEE:  Architectural Record (vol. 152) August 1972, 81-90.

19.    Walker Art Center; Minneapolis, MN; 1971.   A mannerly backdrop for the art it houses and a harmonious neighbor for Ralph Rapson's Guthrie Theater (q. v. ) with which it shares a glass-walled entrance, it has been called "a minimal sculpture inside and out. " Associate in charge:  Alistair M. Bevington.   Engineers:  Paul Weidlinger, and Meyer, Borgman & Johnson (structural); Gausman & Moore (mechanical/electrical).   HONORS:  AIA Honor Award, 1972.   SEE:  Design Quarterly (no. 81) 1971, whole issue.   Architectural Record (vol. 150) July 1971, 34.

S.  B.  BARNES  see  KISTNER,  WRIGHT & WRIGHT; EDWARD H. FICKETT; S. B. BARNES

DONALD BARTHELME

20.    West Columbia Elementary School; West Columbia, TX; 1952. "Neighborhoods" of classrooms oriented around courtyards, airy patterns of exposed steel joists, and ingenious use of colorful and varied materials characterize this cheerful and unusual school. Structural engineer:  Walter B. Moore; contractor:  Fisher Construction Co.   HONORS:  Top award, Texas Society of Architects exhibit, State Fair, 1952.   SEE:  Architectural Forum (vol. 97) October 1952, 102-109.

FRED BASSETTI

21.    Ridgeway Men's Dormitories, Phase 3, Western Washington State College; Bellingham, WA; 1966.   Twenty-six suite-towers progressing down a steep and heavily wooded hillside provide housing and lounge facilities for 450 students.   Each room has its own private outdoor entrance via a stairway or bridge.   Engineers:  Norman Jacobson & Associates (structural); Richard M. Stern (mechnical).   Landscape architects:  Richard Haag Associates.   HONORS:  PA Design Citation, 1965; AIA Honor Award, 1967.   SEE:  Progressive Architecture (vol. 46) January 1965, [126]-170.  AIA Journal (vol. 47) June 1967, 44-[64].

## WELTON BECKET

22. Kaiser Center; Oakland, CA; 1960. This landmark on the shores of Lake Merritt is actually a complex of buildings dominated by a gleaming, 28-story office tower whose faces curve in a dramatic arc. Featuring materials manufactured by Kaiser companies, its curtain wall combines natural finish aluminum frame, gray glass, and gold anodized aluminum panels. Engineers: Murray Erick Associates (structural); Dames & Moore (soil mechanics). Landscape architect: Osmundson & Staley. Contractor: Robert E. McKee General Contractor, Inc. SEE: Architectural Record (vol. 128) December 1960, 117-122.

23. North Carolina Mutual Life Insurance Company; Durham, NC; 1965. Headquarters for the largest black-owned insurance company in the United States, this imposing office building gains symbolic strength from an interplay of massive vertical columns and broad horizontal Vierendeel trusses. Structurally innovative, it was the first to use segmental post-tensioned construction in a tall building. Associated architect: M. A. Ham Associates. Structural/mechanical/electrical engineers: Seelye, Stevenson, Value & Knecht. Landscape architect: Richard C. Bell Associates. SEE: Progressive Architecture (vol. 47) April 1966, 222-226. Concrete (vol. 3) September 1969, 356-359. Progressive Architecture (vol. 46) September 1965, 166-171.

24. Southland Center; Dallas, TX; 1959. Here the 42-story Southland Life office tower and the 28-story, 600-room Sheraton-Dallas Hotel soar above a terrazzo-paved and attractively planted plaza. Through connections under and above the plaza, they offer "bulk space" on their lower floors for convention use. Consulting architect: Mark Lemmon. Structural engineers: Murray Erick Associates. Consulting mechanical engineers: Zumwalt & Vinther. General contractor: J. W. Bateson Co. HONORS: AISC Award of Excellence, 1960. SEE: Architectural Forum (vol. 111) August 1959, 94-101.

## WELTON BECKET and J. E. STANTON

25. Police Facilities Building, Civic Center; Los Angeles, CA; 1955. Occupying a full city block, this building comprises an information center, offices, a laboratory, an auditorium and a jail. The richly finished main lobby features a 36-foot long glass mosaic mural designed and executed by Joe Young. Director of design: Maynard Woodard. Engineers: Murray Erick and Paul E. Jeffers (struc-

tural); Ralph E. Phillips, Inc. (mechanical/electrical). Associated general contractors: Ford J. Twaits Co. and Morrison-Knudsen. HONORS: AIA Merit Award, 1956. SEE: Progressive Architecture (vol. 37) March 1956, 108-115, 145.

## WILLIAM S. BECKETT

26. William Beckett's office; Los Angeles, CA; 1951? When this young architect gutted a former boys' club and, at modest cost, transformed it into a simple yet elegant space for his offices, the results caught the fancy of architects around the world. HONORS: AIA Honor Award, 1952. SEE: Architectural Forum (vol. 94) June 1951, 138-140.

## HERBERT BECKHARD see MARCEL BREUER and HERBERT BECKHARD

## PIETRO BELLUSCHI
Winner, AIA Gold Medal, 1972

27. Equitable Savings and Loan Building; Portland, OR; 1948. This trim, compact office building, 12 stories high originally and later 13, set styles for hundreds that came after. It was the first to be sheathed in aluminum, the first to employ double-glazed window panels, and the first to be completely sealed and fully air conditioned. Mechanical engineer: J. Donald Kroeker. General contractor: Ross B. Hammond. SEE: Architectural Forum (vol. 89) September 1948, 98-106. Architectural Forum (vol. 128) June 1968, [40]-[45].

28. Juilliard School of Music, Lincoln Center; New York, NY; 1969 (Illus. 4). A complex building that contains four theaters as well as classrooms, studios, and other school facilities. The 960-1026 seat Juilliard Theater has a movable ceiling which adjusts to three positions within a seven-foot range. Its neighbors are Alice Tully Hall (1096 seats), Paul Recital Hall (277 seats), and a small Drama Workshop. Associated architects: Eduardo Catalano and Helge Westermann. Engineers: Paul Weidlinger (structural); Jaros, Baum & Bolles (mechanical/electrical). Stage design consultant: Jean Rosenthal Associates, Inc. Acoustical consultant: Heinrich Keilholz. Contractor: Walsh Construction Company. HONORS:

ALICE TULLY HALL

Bard Award, 1970.   SEE: Architectural Record (vol. 147) January 1970, [121]-[130].  Progressive Architecture (vol. 51) December 1970, 55, 65-72.

## BELT, LEMMON & LO; JOHN CARL WARNECKE

29.   State Capitol; Honolulu, HI; 1969.   Openness is the theme of this gracious and dignified statehouse; it is built, with rings of verandahs, around a great courtyard which itself has no walls at street level on two sides.   Local natural features--ancient banyan trees and volcanic mountains--are said to have suggested other design elements:   stately columns and a curved, fluted roof.   Architect in charge of design:  John Carl Warnecke.   Engineers:  Donald T. Lo (structural); Soderholm, Sorensen & Associates (mechanical). Landscape architect:  Richard Tongg.   General contractor:  Reed & Martin, Inc.   HONORS:  PA Design Citation, 1962.   SEE: Architectural Record (vol. 145) May 1969, 117-128.

## GUNNAR BIRKERTS

30.   Federal Reserve Bank of Minneapolis; Minneapolis, MN; 1973.   Here is an engineering tour de force, an office building built like a bridge, with a column-free span of 275 feet.   Framed by its two titanic concrete towers, a sleekly paved plaza lies underneath; protected facilities for security operation are housed beneath the plaza.   Project director:  Charles Fleckenstein.   Engineers: Skilling, Helle, Christiansen, Robertson (structural); Shannon & Wilson (foundation); Jaros, Baum & Bolles (mechanical/electrical). Landscape architects:  Charles Wood & Associates.   General contractor:  Knutson Construction Co.   HONORS:  AISC Architectural Award of Excellence, 1974.   SEE: Architectural Record (vol. 154) November 1973, 105-116.   Y. Futagawa, ed., Gunnar Birkerts & Associates:  IBM Information Systems Center ... Federal Reserve Bank....   (Global Architecture, no. 31.)  Tokyo:  A.D.A. Edita, 1974.

31.   Fisher Administrative Center, University of Detroit; Detroit, MI; 1967. Three architecturally contrasting areas of this building house distinctly different activities.   Its rambling podium of a ground floor

[Opposite:] 4.   Juilliard School of Music.   Pietro Belluschi.   Photo: © Ashod Kassabian 1981.

is devoted to direct services to students; above this base, a lozenge-shaped structure with windows shaded by ranks of vertical fins contains four floors of offices and, in turn, is topped by an executive penthouse which offers views unimpeded by fins. Principal, project administrator: Almon Durkee; associate for design: Keith Brown. Engineers: Holforty, Widrig, O'Neill Associates (structure); Siegel, Swiech & Associates (mechanical). Landscape architects: Johnson, Johnson & Roy. General contractor: Utley-James Corporation. SEE: Architectural Record (vol. 142) July 1967, 109-[114].

32. IBM Sterling Forest Information Systems Center; Sterling Forest, NY; 1972. Designed to house computer operations for IBM's internal control and planning, this facility contrasts sharply with its woodland setting. A "piece of minimal graphic sculpture," its smooth skin is a combination of polished aluminum panels and glass separated by bands of red-orange enameled metal. Designer: Algimantas Bublys and D. Bartley Guthrie. Engineers: Skilling-Helle-Christiansen-Robertson (structural); Hoyem Associates (mechanical/electrical). HONORS: PA Design Citation, 1971. SEE: Progressive Architecture (vol. 53) December 1972, 50-[55]. Y. Futagawa, ed., Gunnar Birkerts & Associates: IBM Information Systems Center ... Federal Reserve Bank.... (Global Architecture, no. 31.) Tokyo: A.D.A. Edita, 1974.

33. Library and two dormitories, Tougaloo College; Tougaloo, MS; 1973. Built on shifting clay, these trim, modular buildings rest on columns well above the ground and are supported on deep foundations of drilled and belled concrete caissons. They were designed in the 1960's as part of an ambitious master plan for this small black college but by the mid-1970's when they were finally completed, further expansion of the campus seemed unlikely. Project director: Charles Fleckenstein. Engineers: Robert M. Darvas & Associates (structural); Hoyem Associates (mechanical/electrical). Contractor: Frazier-Morton Construction Company. SEE: Architectural Record (vol. 144) October 1968, 129-144. Architectural Record (vol. 154) November 1973, 105-116.

34. Lincoln Elementary School; Columbus, IN; Building: 1967; landscaping, 1968? (Illus. 5). A compact, beautifully detailed school, hidden from sight behind a circle of trees, it can be used after school hours for community programs and as a public park. Associate for design: Harold Van Dine. Supervising architects: Siece, Inc. Landscape architects: Johnson, Johnson & Roy. Engineers: Holforty, Widrig, O'Neill & Assoc. (structural); Hoyem, Basso & Adams (mechanical). General contractor: Dunlap Construction Co. HONORS: AIA Honor Award, 1970; Bartlett Award, 1970. SEE: Architectural Forum (vol. 127) November 1967, [48]-[53]. AIA Journal (vol. 53) June 1970, 79-93.

5.  Lincoln Elementary School.   Gunnar Birkerts.
    Photo:  Balthazar Korab

---

WILLIAM N. BREGER

---

35.  Civic Center Synagogue; New York, NY; 1967.   Three boldly curving
     concrete shells shape this small yet striking downtown synagogue.
     The windowless front wall of its sanctuary seems to float above its
     quiet entrance court.   Engineers:  Paul Gugliotta (structural); Bat-
     lan & Oxman (mechanical).   Landscape architect:  M. Paul Fried-
     berg.   Contractor:  Sherry Construction Corporation.   HONORS:
     AIA Honor Award, 1968.   SEE:  Architectural Forum (vol. 127)
     October 1967, [64]-[69].

BREGMAN & HAMANN  see  ZEIDLER PARTNERSHIP; BREGMAN & HAMANN

MARCEL BREUER
Winner, AIA Gold Medal, 1968

36. Dormitory, Vassar College; Poughkeepsie, NY; 1950.  Designed for cooperative living and supplied with ample kitchen facilities, its bedrooms are elevated above ground giving them privacy and providing covered outdoor areas for pingpong tables, bikes and unimpeded views.  SEE:  Architectural Record (vol. 111) January 1952, 127-134.

37. Priory of the Annunciation; Bismarck, ND; 1963.  A distinctive geometric, 100-foot high bell tower sets off a complex of fieldstone, brick and concrete buildings, linked by walkways, housing a Benedictine convent and a preparatory school for girls.  Of particular interest:  the starkly striking main chapel.  Associated local architects:  Traynor & Hermanson.  Structural engineers: Johnston-Sahlman Co.  Structural consultant for chapel:  Paul Weidlinger.  Mechanical engineers:  Gausman & Moore.  General contractors:  Meisner Anderson Co., first stage; Anderson, Guthrie & Carlson, second stage.  SEE:  Architectural Record (vol. 134) December 1963, 95-102.

MARCEL BREUER and HERBERT BECKHARD

38. St. Francis de Sales Church; Muskegon, MI; 1967.  Striated concrete walls that swoop into surprising trapezoids and curves shape the exterior of this church.  The sanctuary, spanned by a system of rigid concrete arches, seats 1200 and features a chapel which, when specially lit, can serve as a second altar.  Engineers:  Paul Weidlinger (structural); Stinard, Piccirillo & Brown (mechanical). Acoustical consultants:  Goodfriend, Ostergaard Associates.  General contractor:  M. A. Lombard & Son.  HONORS:  AIA Honor Award, 1973; AIA Bicentennial List, 1 nomination.  SEE:  Architectural Record (vol. 142) November 1967, 130-[137].

MARCEL BREUER and HAMILTON SMITH

39.  St. John's Abbey; Collegeville, MN; various dates.  Breuer submitted
     the master plan for this Benedictine monastery-campus in 1954.
     By 1961, three buildings were complete: one student dormitory, a
     monastic wing, and a monumental church, one of the finest religious
     structures of modern times, its baptistry surmounted by a high
     banner-bell tower.  Added subsequently: a library, science center,
     more dorms, and an ecumenical visitors center.  Engineers:
     Johnston-Sahlman Co. (structural); Gausman & Moore (mechanical).
     HONORS: AIA Merit Award, 1962.  SEE: Architectural Record
     (vol. 130) November 1961, [132]-142.  Architectural Forum (vol.
     128) May 1968, 40-[57].

40.  Whitney Museum of American Art; New York, NY; 1966.  This dis-
     tinctive museum makes the most of its small corner site.  Upper
     floors, affording maximum gallery space within, cantilever outward
     importantly over its shadowy forecourt; seven windows--irregularly
     spaced trapezoids that vary in size--mark its granite facade like
     symbolic eyes.  Consulting architect: Michael Irving.  Engineers:
     Paul Weidlinger (structural); Werner, Jensen & Korst (mechanical).
     General contractor: HRH Construction Corporation.  HONORS:
     Bard Award, 1968; AIA Honor Award, 1970; Bartlett Award, 1970.
     SEE: Architectural Forum (vol. 125) September 1966, 80-85.
     AIA Journal (vol. 67) September 1978, 40-47.

BRODSKY, HOPF & ADLER  see  HELLMUTH, OBATA & KASSABAUM;
     BRODSKY, HOPF & ADLER

BROOKS, BARR, GRAEBER & WHITE  see  SKIDMORE, OWINGS &
     MERRILL; BROOKS, BARR, GRAEBER & WHITE

JEROME R. BUTLER, JR.
     City Architect, Chicago Dept. of Public Works

41.  Navy Pier Restoration; Chicago, IL; 1976.  Fronting on Lake Michigan
     and originally built (1916) to the design of Charles S. Frost, in the
     Twenties it not only accommodated pleasure boats and outdoor

amusements but boasted a 3500-seat concert hall. Much deterio-
rated thereafter, its massive restoration involved structural repair,
unsealing and expansion of skylight areas, landscaping, and construction of a solar space- and water-heating system. Engineers:
Bureau of Engineering (Louis Koncza, chief engineer). Consultants:
Environmental Systems Design, Inc. (mechanical); Robert H. Samuel & Associates (plumbing). General contractor: Bureau of Construction. HONORS: Chicago AIA Distinguished Buildings Award,
1976; AIA Honor Award for Extended Use, 1977; Bartlett Award,
1977. SEE: Architectural Record (vol. 161) March 1977, [107]-
114.

CARSON, LUNDIN & SHAW
Subsequent name of firm: CARSON, LUNDIN & THORSON.

42. Manufacturers Hanover Trust Company Operations Building; New York,
NY; 1968 (Illus. 6). Behind an intriguing facade that with only the
narrowest slits for windows suggests an IBM card, this building
accommodates computers and other business machines that process
paper work for New York's financial district. Partner in charge
of design: Arvin Shaw III. Engineers: Edwards & Hjorth (structural); Meyer, Strong & Jones (mechanical). General contractor:
George A. Fuller Co. HONORS: AISC Architectural Award of Excellence, 1970. SEE: Architectural Forum (vol. 132) January-
February 1970, 62-67.

CAUDILL ROWLETT SCOTT
Winner of the AIA's Architectural Firm Award, 1972. This firm is
better known currently as CRS.

43. Fodrea Community School; Columbus, IN; 1973. Parents and kids,
administrators and teachers helped design this school. Ramps,
slides and tunnels are incorporated in its two-level open plan; its
exposed structural and mechanical systems, painted in bright colors, form major design elements. Project manager: Truitt B.
Garrison; director of design: Paul A. Kennon; technologist: D.
Wayne McDonnell. General contractor: Repp & Mundt. HONORS:
AISC Architectural Award of Excellence, 1975. SEE: Progressive
Architecture (vol. 55) May 1974, [84]-[87].

44. Jesse H. Jones Hall for the Performing Arts; Houston, TX; 1966.
This theater's superb acoustics, movable ceiling and formidably
flexible seating arrangements have led it to be called "the most

6. Manufacturers Hanover Trust Company Operations Building.
Carson, Lundin & Shaw.
Photo: Ezra Stoller (Esto)

sophisticated building of its kind. " It can seat as many as 3000, but for chamber music and plays, its balcony and rear orchestra areas can be screened off and the orchestra pit and orchestra shell can be repositioned. Engineers: Walter Moore (structural); Bernard Johnson Engineers, Inc. (mechanical/electrical). Acoustical consultants: Bolt, Beranek & Newman. Theater design-engineering consultant: George C. Izenour. General contractor: George A. Fuller Co. HONORS: AIA Honor Award, 1967. SEE: Architectural Record (vol. 141) February 1967, [114]-[121].

45. San Angelo Central High School; San Angelo, TX; 1958. A big school housed in a dozen buildings, all but one air-conditioned, on an ample campus, it is graced by a man-made lake, a large swimming pool, snack bars and appealing walks--yet it was constructed on a minimal budget. Associate architect: Max D. Lovett. Engineers: Edward F. Nye (structural); J. W. Hall, Jr. (mechanical/electrical). Landscape architect: Robert F. White. General contractor: Rose Construction Co. HONORS: AIA Merit Award, 1959; AIA Bicentennial List, 1 nomination. SEE: Architectural Forum (vol. 109) November 1958, 110-123.

CAUDILL ROWLETT SCOTT; DALTON, VAN DIJK, JOHNSON

46. Edwin J. Thomas Hall of Performing Arts, University of Akron; Akron, OH; 1973. By movement of its ceiling alone, this hall can shrink in space from 3000 seats to 2400 to 900 and still retain its fine acoustics. Outside, framed by garden terraces and angular, many leveled hard-landscaping, it is "an insistently abstract arrangement of geometric shapes. " Job captain: Charles Lawrence. Associated architects: R. M. Ginsert & Assoc. Engineers: Dick Ginsert (structural); Scheeser & Buckley (mechanical). Theater design consultant: George C. Izenour Associates; acoustical consultant: Vern O. Knudsen. General contractor: Mosser Construction. HONORS: AIA Bicentennial List, 1 nomination. SEE: Architectural Forum (vol. 139) December 1973, 58-65.

VICTOR CHRIST-JANER

47. James F. Lincoln Library, Lake Erie College; Painesville, OH; 1966/1967. Many cubist touches here. Outside, a variety of aluminum-faced regular polyhedrons seem to float over the recessed concrete base; inside, both natural and artificial illumination come from blocky skylight boxes supplemented by lightwells.

Engineers and general contractor: The Austin Co. HONORS: R. S. Reynolds Memorial Award. SEE: Architectural Forum (vol. 127) July-August 1967, 46-[75], [78]-[85], [90]-[97].

---

## MARIO CIAMPI

---

48. Fernando Rivera Elementary School; Daly City, CA; 1960. A small, one-story school that nestles under a sawtoothed roof of angled plywood plates. Its 12 classrooms, kindergarten, library and related facilities are dispersed into five clusters bounded by courts of varying size. Associate: Paul Reiter. Engineers: Isadore Thompson (structural); Van Dament & Darmsted (mechanical). General contractor: Midstate Construction Co. HONORS: AIA Honor Award, 1961. SEE: Architectural Forum (vol. 114) April 1961, 114-117.

49. University Art Museum, University of California; Berkeley, CA; 1970. When completed it was the country's largest university art museum. Located just off campus, its casual concrete ramps lure the passerby into its galleries; its terraces overlook a sunny sculpture garden. Design associates: Richard L. Jorasch and Ronald E. Wagner. Engineers: Isadore Thompson (structural); K. T. Belotelkin & Assoc. (mechanical). Landscape architects: Mario J. Ciampi & Associates. General contractor: Rothschild & Rafin, Inc. SEE: Architectural Record (vol. 152) July 1972, [97]-[112].

50. Westmoor High School; Daly City, CA; 1957/1958. Lively metal sculpture and a colorful porcelain enamel mural adorn this inexpensively-built high school--designed, factory style, in low, 30-foot square bays--which also features glass-walled perimeter corridors and a pleasantly landscaped central mall. Associates: Allyn C. Martin, Paul Reiter. Engineers: Isadore Thompson (structural); Buonaccorsi & Murray (mechanical). Landscape architect: Lawrence Halprin. General contractor: Theodore G. Meyer & Sons. HONORS: AIA Honor Award, 1958. SEE: Architectural Forum (vol. 108) May 1958, 120-125.

---

## CORLETT & SPACKMAN

---

51. Blyth Arena; Squaw Valley, CA; 1959. Tent shaped, this stadium built for the 1960 Winter Olympics is open on one side to sunshine and the ski-jumping hill. Its roof is suspended, like a bridge, from cables strung over tapered steel masts and tied down to

concrete piers. Associated architects: Kitchen & Hunt. Engineers: H. J. Brunnier, John M. Sardis (structural); Vandament & Darmsted (mechanical/electrical); Punnett, Parez & Hutchison (civil). Contractors: Diversified Builders, Inc.; York Corp.; Independent Iron Works, Inc. HONORS: PA Design Award, 1958; AIA Honor Award, 1960. SEE: Architectural Forum (vol. 112) February 1960, 104-106.

COSSUTA & PONTE see I. M. PEI; COSSUTA & PONTE

CRS see CAUDILL ROWLETT SCOTT

CURTIS & DAVIS

52. Immaculate Conception Church, Marrero, LA. 1957. The steeply vaulted nave and unusual, undulating ceiling of this concrete-and-steel Roman Catholic church focus attention on the sanctuary and main altar. A double prizewinner, its design was modified substantially after it won its award from Progressive Architecture. Associated architect: Harrison Schouest; associate-in-charge: Walter J. Rooney, Jr. Engineers: Walter E. Blessey, Jr. (structural); Favrot, Guillot, Sullivan & Vogt (mechanical/electrical). General contractor: Gervais F. Favrot. HONORS: PA Award Citation, 1956; AIA Merit Award, 1958. SEE: Progressive Architecture (vol. 39) June 1958, 119-136.

53. New Orleans Public Library; New Orleans, LA; 1958. Here's a library that, like a department store, invites the patron to come in and shop around! Inside, thanks to lavish use of glass, the eye is led from one area to another while enjoying views of the sky and attractive outdoor terraces. Outside, above ground level, the glass structure is enveloped by a lacy sunscreen that reduces glare and heat. Associated architects: Goldstein, Parham & Labouisse; Fravrot, Reed, Mathes & Bergman. Mechanical engineer: Joseph Pazon. General contractor: R. P. Farnsworth & Co. HONORS: PA Design Award, 1957. SEE: Progressive Architecture (vol. 41) April 1960, 152-155. Interiors (vol. 126) February 1967, [100]-147.

54. Superdome; New Orleans, LA; 1975. A giant stadium in the heart of the city which, thanks to a unique system of movable stands, can

be used not only for sports and cultural events but also for trade shows and conventions. Built on a 55-acre site, its golden dome covers 10 acres and rises to a height of 25 stories. Associated architects: Edward B. Silverstein & Associates; Nolan, Norman & Nolan. Engineers: Sverdrup & Parcel. HONORS: AIA Bicentennial List, 1 nomination. SEE: Interiors (vol. 133) August 1973, 94-99. Indian Institute of Architects Journal (vol. 40) April-June 1974, 16-19.

DALTON, VAN DIJK, JOHNSON  see  CAUDILL ROWLETT SCOTT; DALTON, VAN DIJK, JOHNSON

DANIEL, MANN, JOHNSON & MENDENHALL

55. Comsat Laboratories; Clarksburg, MD; 1970. A building complex with a glittering aluminum exterior, sited on 210 rolling acres, where Communications Satellite Corporation employees perform research and produce prototype satellites. Facilities include labs, offices, an auditorium, cafeteria, library, and a satellite assembly area. Director of design: Cesar Pelli; design associate: Philo Jacobsen; partner-in-charge: S. Kenneth Johnson. Landscape architect: Lester Collins. General contractor: J. W. Bateson. HONORS: PA Design Citation, 1968. SEE: Progressive Architecture (vol. 51) August 1970, [70]-[75]. John Pastier, Cesar Pelli. New York: Whitney Library of Design, 1980.

RICHARD DATTNER  see  DAVIS, BRODY; RICHARD DATTNER

DAVIS, BRODY
    In 1975, this firm won the AIA's Architectural Firm Award; in 1977, it won the AIA's Louis Sullivan Award.

56. Riverbend Houses; New York, NY; 1969. Here, despite a tight budget, 624 apartments, 2 spacious playgrounds and 10,000 square feet of commercial space have been stylishly fitted into a small, awkward site on the banks of the Harlem River. Ribbons of walkways and platforms bridge intervening streets; high-rise towers alternate with

medium-rise duplex blocks. Senior associate-in-charge: Brian Smith; project coordinator: Walter Beattie. Engineers: Wiesenfeld & Leon (structural); Wald & Zigas (mechanical/electrical). Site work: Coffey & Levine and M. Paul Friedberg & Assoc. Builder-sponsor: HRH Construction Corp. HONORS: Bard Award, 1969. SEE: Architectural Forum (vol. 131) July/August 1969, 44-55.

57. Waterside; New York, NY; 1975 (Illus. 7). High rise, brick-sheathed apartment building with 1440 housing units built over the East River on specially designed piles. Other features of this development include four acres of neatly detailed plazas, a river-edge promenade, ample commercial space, and a 900-car garage. Associate: John Lebduska; project architect: Herbert Levine; project designer: Ian Ferguson. Engineers: Robert Rosenwasser (structural/soils); Cosentini Associates (mechanical/electrical). General contractor: HRH Construction Corp. HONORS: Bard Award, 1975; AIA Honor Award, 1976; Bartlett Award, 1976. SEE: Architectural Record (vol. 159) March 1976, 119-124.

---

DAVIS, BRODY; RICHARD DATTNER

---

58. Estee Lauder Laboratories; Melville, NY; first stage: 1967; second stage: 1971. Plans for this streamlined cosmetics plant situated alongside the Long Island Expressway allowed for expansion. In 1971, when its size was doubled, it became longer and sleeker--and a top prizewinner. Project architect: Richard L. Carpenter. Engineers: Goldreich, Page & Thropp (structural); Wald & Zigas (mechanical). Landscape architect: A. E. Bye & Associates. General contractor: W. J. Barney Corp. HONORS: AIA Award, 1971. SEE: Architectural Forum (vol. 134) April 1971, 19-[41].

---

JORGE DEL RIO and EDUARDO LOPEZ

---

59. Housing for the Elderly; Cidra Municipality, Puerto Rico; 1968. Sixteen residential units--concrete plastered with white stucco--cluster around small, vehicle-free plazas on a tropical hillside. Farther down the hill, garden lots are provided for the use of the residents. Project architect: Eduardo Lopez. Engineers: Narciso Padilla (structural); Jorge del Rio (mechanical). Landscape architect: Jorge del Rio. General contractor: Alvarez & Zabala. HONORS: PA Design Citation, 1967; AIA Honor Award, 1977. SEE: Progressive Architecture (vol. 54) June 1973, 120-121. AIA Journal (vol. 66) May 1977, [28]-49.

7.  Waterside.  Davis, Brody.
    Photo:  © Ashod Kassabian 1981

VERNON DEMARS  see  JOSEPH ESHERICK; DONALD OLSEN; VERNON DEMARS

DESMOND & LORD  see  PAUL RUDOLPH; DESMOND & LORD

WALT DISNEY
Creator of original concept and entrepreneur

60. Disneyland; Anaheim, CA; 1955.  Visitors to this 160-acre recreation-al complex find themselves first in the Main Street of a dream American town of the 1890's reproduced in loving detail at five-eighths scale.  Nearby are other idealized settings:  Tomorrowland, Fantasyland, Frontierland and Adventureland.  In a wry 1965 arti-cle, Charles Moore (q.v.) called Disneyland "the most important single piece of construction in the West in the past several dec-ades."  Engineering firm:  J. S. Hamel.  Landscape development: Evans & Reeves Nurseries.  HONORS:  AIA Bicentennial List, 1 nomination.  SEE:  Travel (vol. 104) July 1955, 16-19.  Landscape Architecture (vol. 46) April 1956, 125-136.  Perspecta (no. 9/10) 1965, 57-106.

CHARLES DUBOSE

61. Constitution Plaza; Hartford, CT; 1963.  This downtown business cen-ter built on the site of a former slum comprises several imposing office buildings, a shopping mall, a hotel and two garages, all set around a handsomely landscaped plaza.  DuBose's responsibilities included site planning, basic design of the overall project, and gen-eral design coordination.  He also served as architect for the North and South Garages, East and West Commercial Buildings, Research Center and Brokerage House.  Associated architects for 100 Consti-tution Plaza:  Charles DuBose and Emery Roth & Sons.  Associated architects for Hotel America:  Charles DuBose and Curtis & Davis. Architects for Broadcast House:  Fulmer & Bowers.  Architects for One Constitution Plaza (Connecticut Bank and Trust Co. Building): Kahn & Jacobs (for the owner) and Carson, Lundin & Shaw (for the bank).  HONORS:  AIA Merit Award, 1964.  SEE:  Architectural Record (vol. 135) March 1964, 178-[187].  SEE ALSO:  Phoenix

Mutual Life Insurance Co. Building, by Harrison & Abramovitz, entry no. 106. (Though not controlled by DuBose's site plan, this nearby office tower coordinates well with it.)

---

## EDWARDS & PORTMAN
See also JOHN PORTMAN.

---

62. Hyatt Regency Hotel; Atlanta, GA; 1967. The breathtaking 21-story, skylighted atrium/lobby of this 800-room hotel has set the fashion for many another hotel--some designed by Portman, some by others. This giant courtyard, 140 feet across, has vine-covered cantilevered balconies on all four sides; they serve as corridors for the guest rooms, all of which also have outside balconies. Designer: John Portman. HONORS: AIA Bicentennial List, 3 nominations. SEE: Interior Design (vol. 38) September 1967, 136-[149]. L'Architecture Française (no. 303-304) November-December 1967, 12-[14]. Architectural Forum (vol. 130) April 1969, 42-[51].

---

## CRAIG ELLWOOD

---

63. Art Center College of Design; Pasadena, CA; 1976. A one- and two-story steel and glass structure, with exposed steel columns and beams, that spans 192 feet across a ravine. Since on either side, where it rises two stories, much of its first floor lies below ground level, the Center looks like a one-story pavilion on a raised platform. Consultant: Norman Epstein (structural); Eli Silon & Associates (mechanical/electrical); Alfred Caldwell/Erik Katzmaier (landscape). General contractor: Swinerton & Walberg. HONORS: PA Design Citation, 1976. SEE: Progressive Architecture (vol. 58) August 1977, 62-[65].

64. Scientific Data Systems, Inc.; El Segundo, CA; 1966. A sprawling computer plant (560' x 464') that's been hailed as a distinguished piece of architecture yet was built quickly and cheaply. Clever engineering makes optimum use of steel trusses; steel columns are left free-standing outside the perimeter of the building. Engineers: Mackintosh & Mackintosh (structural); Stanley Feuer (mechanical). General contractor: C. L. Peck. Landscape architect: Warren Waltz. SEE: Architectural Forum (vol. 125) November 1966, [70]-[77]. Lotus (vol. 4) 1967-1968, [15]-[123]. Arts and Architecture (vol. 83) November 1966, [28]-[31].

ERICKSON/MASSEY

65. Expo '67 theme buildings; Montreal, Canada; 1967. Designed to show advanced technology in wood, the exhibit's central building, "Man in the Community," was a pagoda-style pyramid constructed of 37 layers of composite Glulam and plywood beams combined to give the effect of a giant lattice. A smaller building nearby, housing "Man and His Health," echoed the central building's lines. Engineers: Janos J. Baracs (structural); Bouthiellette & Parizeau (mechanical/electrical). Special consultant in structural systems: Jeffrey Lindsay. HONORS: Massey Medal for Architecture, 1970 Awards Competition. SEE: Architecture Canada (vol. 43) July 1966, 29-52. Architectural Design (vol. 37) July 1967, 333-[347].

66. Simon Fraser University; Burnaby, British Columbia, Canada; 1965. Sited atop a mountain just outside Vancouver, a series of harmonizing concrete buildings are linked by wide, weather-protected spaces. Axial to the campus, designed for up to 18,000 students, is a huge, multi-purpose covered mall. Planning, design concept of all buildings, design coordination, site development and landscaping: Erickson/Massey. Within this framework, the following architects prepared preliminary designs, working drawings, and supervised individual buildings: Zoltan S. Kiss (academic quadrangle); Duncan McNab (theatre, gymnasium and swimming pool); Rhone & Iredale (science complex); Robert F. Harrison (library). SEE: Architectural Forum (vol. 123) December 1965, [13]-[21]. Canadian Architect (vol. 11) February 1966, whole issue.

JOSEPH ESHERICK
See also entry no. 189.

67. Adlai E. Stevenson College, University of California; Santa Cruz, CA; residence and academic buildings, 1966; library 1968; music practice rooms, 1975. There's a "hang loose" look to this campus within a campus: three complexes of white-walled, red-roofed buildings with lots of unexpected juts and angles, amiably tucked into a wooded site. It has won high honors for its "playful forms set with variety in a handsome grove of trees." Engineers: Rutherford & Chekene (structural); G. L. Gendler & Assoc. (mechanical/electrical). Landscape architects: Lawrence Halprin & Assoc. General contractor: Williams & Burrows. HONORS: AIA Honor Award, 1968; Award of Merit, Library Buildings 1970 Award Program, AIA, et al. SEE: Progressive Architecture (vol. 48) November 1967, [138]-145. AIA Journal (vol. 54) August 1970, 31-33.

68. The Cannery: San Francisco, CA; 1968. A clever renovation that created a mecca for tourists and other shoppers. The old, brick Del Monte Cannery, conveniently located near Fisherman's Wharf, was gutted and entirely rebuilt inside, transformed into three levels of varied commercial space served by elevators, an escalator and seven different staircases--all arranged, says Esherick, with "enough turns, zigzags and corners ... to offer at least some hint of a maze." Engineers: Rutherford & Chekene (structural); K. T. Belotekin & Assoc. (mechanical). Landscape architect: Thomas Church. General contractor: Greystone Builders. HONORS: AIA Honor Award, 1970; Bartlett Award, 1970. SEE: Architectural Forum (vol. 128) June 1968, [74]-79.

JOSEPH ESHERICK; DONALD OLSEN; VERNON DEMARS

69. Wurster Hall, College of Environmental Design, University of California; Berkeley, CA; 1965 (Illus. 8). Designed jointly by three members of Berkeley's architecture faculty, this bluntly detailed building with its hatchwork of sunshading concrete slabs and its assertive tower contrasts boldly with its self-effacing, tile-roofed neighbors. Inside, in Brutalist fashion, the ducts and pipes of the mechanical system are left exposed. Engineers: Isadore Thompson (structural); G. L. Gendler & Assoc. (mechanical). General contractor: Rothschild, Raffin & Weirick. SEE: Architectural Forum (vol. 124) January-February 1966, [56]-[63].

EDWARD H. FICKETT see KISTNER, WRIGHT & WRIGHT; EDWARD H. FICKETT; S. B. BARNES

O'NEIL FORD

70. Tower of the Americas; San Antonio, TX; 1968. A 622-foot tower with a slender, ribbed stem, it was built as the centerpiece for the San Antonio HemisFair of 1968 and contains a revolving restaurant, a stationary one and an observation deck. SEE: AIA Journal (vol. 49) April 1968, 48-58. Architectural Forum (vol. 129) October 1968, 84-89.

8. Wurster Hall, University of California, Berkeley. Esherick, Homsey, Dodge & Davis. Photo: Rondal Partridge

ULRICH FRANZEN

71. Alley Theatre; Houston, TX; 1968 (Illus. 9). Graced with curving parapets and topped by turrets that give it an almost medieval look, this building houses two theaters (one seating 800, the other seating 300) separated by a covered driveway and linked below it by shared dressing rooms and areas for the preparation and storage of costumes and sets. Job captain: Keith Kroeger. Associate architects: MacKie & Kamrath. Engineers: Weiskopf & Pickworth (structural); Cosentini Associates (mechanical). Lighting systems and theater equipment: George Izenour. Acoustical consultants: Bolt, Beranek & Newman. General contractor: W. S. Bellows Construction Corp. HONORS: AIA Honor Award, 1972; Bartlett Award, 1972. SEE: Architectural Forum (vol. 130) March 1969, 31-[39]. AIA Journal (vol. 57) May 1972, 31-40. Process: Architecture (no. 8) 1979, 37-74.

72. Barkin, Levin & Co. factory and office building; Long Island City, NY; 1958. Comfortable, efficient quarters for all the processes involved in manufacturing a line of quality women's coats. The ultimate design was based on comprehensive research into storage problems, operations flow, etc. and resulted in a 50 percent saving in space and a 30 percent saving in manufacturing time. Engineers: Seelye, Stevenson, Value & Knecht. Contractors: Schumacher & Forelle. SEE: Architectural Record (vol. 125) February 1959, 197-202. Process: Architecture (no. 8) 1979, 11-36.

73. Bradfield and Emerson Halls, Cornell University; Ithaca, NY; 1968. A 13-story laboratory tower for agricultural research, also known as the Agronomy Building, plus associated facilities. Built of dark red, hard-surfaced brick and with the striking lines of "a very handsome piece of architectural sculpture," its windows are limited to narrow slots in the stairtowers since its interior must be air-controlled. Project manager: Robert Thorson; project architect: Edward Rosen. Consulting landscape architect: George Swanson. Engineers: Weiskopf & Pickworth (structural); Cosentini Associates (mechanical). General contractor: Irwin & Leighton. HONORS: AIA Honor Award, 1970. SEE: Architectural Forum (vol. 129) July/August 1968, 40-53. AIA Journal (vol. 53) June 1970, 79-93. Architecture, Formes, Fonctions (vol. 16) 1971, 333-341.

74. Christensen Hall, University of New Hampshire; Durham, NH; 1970. Clean cut, brick faced residence halls which aim to provide a sense of privacy and individualized living to occupants sharing double rooms. Floor plans vary from one level to another, L-shaped rooms give each student a distinct "nook," and for every dozen rooms there's a communal study/lounge. Associate in charge:

9.  Alley Theatre.  Ulrich Franzen & Associates, Architects.
    Photo:  Ezra Stoller (Esto)

Samuel E. Nylen. Engineers: Garfinkel, Marenberg & Assoc. (structural); John J. Altieri (mechanical/electrical). Contractor: Harvey Construction. HONORS: AIA Honor Award, 1971. SEE: Architectural Record (vol. 148) November 1970, 101-[104].

---

FRY & WELCH  see  PAUL RUDOLPH; FRY & WELCH

---

R. BUCKMINSTER FULLER
  Winner, Royal Gold Medal, 1968; AIA Gold Medal, 1970.

---

75.  Union Tank Car Repair Facility; Baton Rouge, LA; 1958. A maintenance and repair facility for railway tank cars, built in the round to accommodate circular traffic flow patterns fed by a rotating transfer table. When completed it was the largest geodesic dome ever built: 120 feet high, with an unobstructed interior diameter of 384 feet. Creator of fundamental design: R. Buckminster Fuller. Architects and engineers: Battey & Childs. Dome engineers: Synergetics, Inc. Contractor: Nicols Construction Co. HONORS: Fuller, as designer of both the geodesic dome and the Dymaxion house, received five nominations for the AIA Bicentennial List. SEE: Architectural Record (vol. 125) January 1959, 147-170.

---

R. BUCKMINSTER FULLER/FULLER & SADAO

---

76.  U. S. Pavilion, Expo '67; Ile Ste. Hélène, Montreal, Canada; 1967. A giant dome, roughly three quarters of a sphere, designed to look like a lacy filigree weightlessly poised against the sky. Height: 200 feet; spherical diameter: 250 feet. Construction: a space frame of steel pipes enclosing 1900 molded acrylic panels. Associated: Geometrics. Interior platforms and exhibit: Cambridge Seven Associates. Structural engineers: Simpson, Gumpertz & Heger. Associated Canadian architect: George F. Eber. HONORS: AIA Honor Award, 1968. SEE: Architectural Design (vol. 37) July 1967, 333-[347].

## GEDDES, BRECHER & CUNNINGHAM

77. Addition (Pender Laboratory), to Moore School of Electrical Engineering, University of Pennsylvania; Philadelphia, PA; 1958. A laboratory-classroom wing which links two earlier buildings: the Towne School, a turn of the century Jacobean effort, and the Moore School, built along squarer lines in the late twenties. Vigorous in itself, it also articulates well with two adjacent buildings of different scale and character. Engineers: Dorfman & Bloom (structural); J. P. Hartman (mechanical/electrical). General contractor: Joseph R. Farrell, Inc. HONORS: AIA Honor Award, 1960. SEE: Architectural Forum (vol. 110) March 1959, 94-99.

## GEDDES, BRECHER, QUALLS, CUNNINGHAM

78. Faner Hall, Southern Illinois University; Carbondale, IL; 1975/1976 (Illus. 10). A 900-foot long, spinelike megastructure which serves as Humanities and Social Sciences Center on a sprawling, 21,000-student campus. Colonnades echo a nearby strip of woodland and, along with sun baffles, provide shade in the afternoon. Design partner: Robert L. Geddes; design associate: M. Neville Epstein; project architect: John R. De Bello. Mechanical engineering consultants: United Engineers. General contractor: J. L. Simmins Co. HONORS: AIA Honor Award, 1977; Bartlett Award, 1977. SEE: Progressive Architecture (vol. 57) December 1976, 45-49.

79. Police Headquarters Building; Philadelphia, PA; 1962. A police office building of remarkable charm and grace, shaped in a sequence of arcs inside and out. Built of precast concrete, public areas at its center curve outward into almost circular security clusters at either side. Upper floors cantilever out boldly 12 feet from the base. Senior staff architect: Roland A. Gallimore. Engineers: David Bloom and Dr. August E. Komendant (structural); Cronheim & Weger (mechanical/electrical). Acoustical consultants: Bolt, Beranek & Newman. General contractor: Sovereign Construction Co. SEE: Architectural Forum (vol. 118) February 1963, [120]-[125].

## FRANK O. GEHRY

80. Concord Pavilion; Concord, CA; 1975. Here's a fan-shaped, open air

10. Faner Hall, Southern Illinois University. Geddes, Brecher, Qualls, Cunningham.

performing arts center located in Northern California, at the foot
of Mt. Diablo. Seating for 3500 is provided under its roof, an-
other 4500 can be accommodated in a raked, grassy bowl--all set
in a crater-shaped amphitheater. Design team: Frank O. Gehry,
C. Gregory Walsh, Jr., James F. Porter. Engineers: Garfinkel
& Kurily & Assoc. (structural); John Kerr Associates (mechanical);
Irving Schwartz Associates (electrical). Landscape architects and
civil engineers: Sasaki-Walker & Assoc. Consultant: Christopher
Jaffe (acoustics, stage and lighting design). Contractor: F. P.
Lathrop Construction Co. HONORS: AIA Honor Award, 1977;
AISC Architectural Award of Excellence, 1977. SEE: Architec-
tural Record (vol. 159) June 1976, 95-102.

## GIFFELS & ROSSETTI

81. Cobo Hall and Joe Louis Arena; Detroit, MI; 1960. When completed in 1960, this colossus--designed to house the annual National Auto Show--was the world's largest exhibit building. It sprawls nearly 1000 feet over a six-lane expressway, features a rooftop parking lot, and contains 2.2 million square feet of space. Engineers: Giffels & Rossetti, Inc. Contractor: O. W. Burke Co. SEE: Architectural Forum (vol. 113) October 1960, 98-100.

## BRUCE GOFF

82. Hopewell Baptist Church; Edmond, OK; 1953. A teepee-shaped church designed by one of America's most innovative architects to be built by a congregation of oilfield workers--pipe welders, drillers and riggers--and their families. Spidery trusses that suggest an oil derrick support a 12-sided structure faced with corrugated aluminum. Even the pews are made of pipes and planks. Assistant: William H. Wilson. SEE: Architectural Forum (vol. 101) December 1954, 118-131.

## BERTRAND GOLDBERG

83. Health Sciences Center, State University of New York at Stony Brook; Stony Brook, NY; 1976. A steel and concrete megastructure that comprises three huge, connected towers and encloses two million feet of flexible, multi-purpose space. SEE: Inland Architect (vol. 18) January 1974, 20-21. A+U: Architecture and Urbanism (no. 55) July 1975, 73-86. Arthur Drexler, Transformation in Modern Architecture. New York: Museum of Modern Art, 1979.

84. Marina City; Chicago, IL; 1964, plus additions completed 1967 (Illus. 11). When built, this development's two audacious, 60-story, petal-ringed towers were the tallest residential buildings and tallest concrete structures in the world. Twenty stories of parking space are provided on the lower levels of the towers, while space for offices, shops and a marina are supplied in a complex of facilities nearby. Structural consultants: Severud-Perrone-Fischer-Sturm-Conlin-Bandel; Mueser, Rutledge, Wentworth & Johnson; Dr. Ralph Peck. Contractor: James McHugh Construction Co.

11. Marina City. Bertrand Goldberg.
    Photo: Bill Engdahl, Hedrich-Blessing

HONORS: AIA Bicentennial List, 1 nomination. SEE: Architectural Forum (vol. 122) April 1965, [68]-[77].

85. Prentice Women's Hospital and Maternity Center, Northwestern University Downtown Campus; Chicago, IL; 1975. This medical facility features a seven-story tower, shaped like a four-leaf clover, which contains 264 beds arranged in four patient care "villages" per floor. Perched atop a striated stem, it is surrounded at its base by a four-story, rectilinear structure which accommodates admissions, support services, and several specialized treatment units. Engineers: Bertrand Goldberg Associates. Contractor: Paschen-Newburg. SEE: Inland Architect (vol. 18) January 1974, 16-17. Architectural Record (vol. 159) July 1976, 109-124.

---

## GOLEMAN & ROLFE; PIERCE & PIERCE

---

86. Houston Intercontinental Airport, Terminals A and B; Houston, TX; 1968. The first American airport designed for supersonic travel. Its terminals, which offer close-in, efficient access to both autos and planes, reduce passenger walking to a minimum and are linked by a completely automated mini-transit loop. Engineers: Engineers of the Southwest, a joint venture of Lockwood, Andrews & Newman; Bovay Engineers; and Turner, Collie & Braden. Landscape architects: Bishop & Walker and Fred Buxton. Contractor: R. F. Ball Construction Co. SEE: Architectural Record (vol. 144) August 1968, 123-146. Progressive Architecture (vol. 50) September 1969, 92-115.

---

## JOHN GRAHAM

---

87. Space Needle; Seattle, WA; 1962. A 600-foot steel tower built originally for Seattle's World's Fair, Century 21, and retained as part of the civic center. An unmistakable landmark, it features a lofty observation deck and revolving restaurant just under its skyscraper spire. Engineers: John Graham & Co. Design assistant: Victor Steinbreuck. Structural consultant: John K. Minasian. HONORS: AIA Bicentennial List, 1 nomination. SEE: Architectural Record (vol. 130) August 1961, 95-[106]. Architectural Record (vol. 131) June 1962, [141]-[148].

## VICTOR GRUEN

88. Northland Regional Shopping Center; Southfield Township, near Detroit, MI; 1954. The first shopping center designed as a compact "market town" where shoppers, once they have parked their cars, can browse easily through a series of pedestrian malls. Space for 12,000 cars, 1,045,000 sq. ft. of rentable area, 80 shops and one department store. Engineers: Victor Gruen Associates. Associate in charge: Karl van Leuven, Jr. Associated mechanical and electrical engineers: H. E. Beyster & Assoc. Landscape architect: Edward Eichstedt. General contractor: Bryant & Detwiler Co. HONORS: AIA Merit Award, 1954; AIA Bicentennial List, 1 nomination. SEE: Architectural Forum (vol. 100) June 1954, 102-123.

## GRUEN ASSOCIATES

89. Pacific Design Center; Los Angeles, CA; 1976. A six story, earthquake resistant, 750,000 sq. ft. home furnishings market sheathed in vivid blue glass. Though dubbed "the beached whale" and "the blue blimp," its many attractive features include a barrel-vaulted galleria on its top two floors and a huge, handsome circulation cylinder at its south end. Partner in charge of design: Cesar Pelli. Partners in charge of project: Edgardo Contini and Allen Rubenstein; project designer: Miloyko Lazovich; construction coordinator: John Friedman. Landscape consultant: Gustav Molnar. General contractor: Henry C. Beck Co. SEE: Progressive Architecture (vol. 57) October 1976, 78-83. Y. Futagawa, ed., Cesar Pelli/Gruen Associates ... Pacific Design Center.... Text by Kenneth Frampton. (Global Architecture, no. 59.) Tokyo: A. D. A. Edita, 1981.

90. Rainbow Center Mall and Winter Garden; Niagara Falls, NY; 1977 (Illus. 12). A giant, asymmetrical greenhouse, 155 x 175 x 107 feet high, sited as a centerpiece for a downtown pedestrian mall. Beneath its airy web of glass and steel lies a lushly landscaped garden criss-crossed by stairs and catwalks which lead to two fanciful observation towers. Partner in charge: Beda Zwicker; partner in charge of design: Cesar Pelli. Landscape architects: M. Paul Friedberg & Partners. Engineers: DeSimone & Chaplin (structural); Cosentini Assoc. (mechanical/electrical). Contractor: Scrufari-Siegfriend Joint Venture. Interior landscape contractor: The Everett Conklin Cos. HONORS: PA Design Award Citation, 1977; AISC Architectural Award of Excellence, 1978. SEE: Pro-

12. Rainbow Center Mall and Winter Garden. Gruen Associates.
    Photo: Norman McGrath

gressive Architecture (vol. 59) August 1978, 72-81.   Y. Futagawa, ed., Cesar Pelli/Gruen Associates ... Pacific Design Center ... Rainbow Mall and Winter Garden.   Text by Kenneth Frampton. (Global Architecture no. 59.) Tokyo:  A. D. A. Edita, 1981.

## GWATHMEY, HENDERSON & SIEGEL

91.   Dormitory and dining hall, State University of New York; Purchase, NY, 1973.   An 800-student dormitory with a dramatic dining hall that can serve 400.   To provide a sense of intimacy despite its large size, the U-shaped, three-story dorm's many entries divide student accommodations into groups of about 60, 20 to a floor; each floor has its own handsome lounge area.   Associate in charge: Andrew Pettit.   Engineers:  Geiger-Berger (structural); William Kaplan with Langer-Polise (mechanical/electrical).   Landscape architect:  Peter G. Rolland.   Contractor:  Jos. L. Muscarelle, Inc.   HONORS:  AIA Honor Award, 1976.   SEE:  Architecture Plus (vol. 1) May 1973, [32]-[43].   AIA Journal (vol. 65) April 1976, 36-57.

## GWATHMEY SIEGEL

92.   Whig Hall, Princeton University; Princeton, NJ; 1973.   When this fine old home of a debating society--built in the form of a neo-classical temple--was gutted by fire, Gwathmey Siegel renovated it boldly, inserting new concrete slab floor levels to supply additional floor space, and removing one entire side wall to expose the new interior in candid contrast to its marble shell.   Job captain:  Timothy Wood.   Engineers:  David Geiger-Horst Berger (structural); Langer Polise (mechanical).   HONORS:  PA Design Citation, 1973; AIA Honor Award for Extended Use, 1976.   SEE:  Progressive Architecture (vol. 54) June 1973.   AIA Journal (vol. 65) April 1976, 36-57.

## DAVID HAID

93.   Abraham Lincoln Oasis; South Holland, IL; 1968.   Meticulous attention to detail and clarity of line lend distinction to this highway restaurant/rest stop, a weathering steel structure enclosed with bronze-

tinted glass. Built directly across the highway--135 feet clear span plus an additional 45 feet at each end--it is a calm retreat for travelers going either way. Engineers: Weisinger-Holland (structural); Wallace-Migdal (mechanical/electrical). Contractor: Leo Michuda & Son. HONORS: AISC Architectural Award of Excellence, 1968. SEE: Architectural Forum (vol. 129) September 1968, [76]-[79].

## LAWRENCE HALPRIN

94. Civic Auditorium Forecourt; Portland, OR; 1968/1970. A many-leveled, one-block-square extravaganza of waterfalls, stairs that form an irregular outdoor theater, and low mounds planted with maples and oaks--all set off by lighting at night. Partner in charge: Satoru Nishita; project director: Byron McCulley; designer: Angela Danadjieva Tzvetin. Engineers: Gilbert, Forsberg, Diekmann & Schmidt (structural); Beamer/Wilkinson (mechanical/electrical). General contractor: Schrader Construction Co. HONORS: ASLA Honor Award, 1971; AIA Bicentennial List, 2 nominations. SEE: Architectural Forum (vol. 133) October 1970, 56-[59]. Process: Architecture (no. 4) February 1978, 178-184.

HARALSON & MOTT  see  EDWARD DURELL STONE; HARALSON & MOTT

## HARDY HOLZMAN PFEIFFER

95. The Cloisters; Cincinnati, OH; 1970 (Illus. 13). A condominium built on a "precipitous, odd-shaped and constricted" 1.4-acre site, it is a wood-framed structure supported on round timber poles, with fire resistant masonry walls dividing the units. Each of its 17 units enjoys ample space and an attractive view. Consultants: WHB Associates (mechanical); Miller, Tallarico, McNinch & Hoeffel (structural). HONORS: First Honor Award, 1973 Homes for Better Living Program, AIA, et al. SEE: Progressive Architecture (vol. 52) May 1971, [86]-91. House Beautiful (vol. 114) June 1972, [50-55]. House & Home (vol. 44) August 1973, 70-83.

96. Columbus Occupational Health Center; Columbus, IN; 1973. This medical center's interior is enlivened by a colorful display of pipes, coils, bolts and flanges used both functionally and as architectural

13. The Cloisters Condominium. Hardy Holzman Pfeiffer.
Photo: Norman McGrath

ornament. Its exterior is sheathed in two intersecting glazing systems (one black, the other mirrored) while, overhead, light flows in from two long, intersecting mirrored skylights. Project architects: Michael Ross, Marvin Wiehe, C. E. John Way, Patrick Stanigar. Engineers: Arthur Miller Associates (structural); Ziel-Blossom Associates (mechanical/electrical). Landscape consultant: Dan Kiley. General contractor: Repp & Mundt, Inc. HONORS: AIA Honor Award, 1976; Bartlett Award, 1976. SEE: <u>Architectural Record</u> (vol. 158) October 1975, 95-102.

97. Robert S. Marx Theater, the Playhouse in the Park; Cincinnati, OH; 1968. A 672-seat playhouse set on a grassy knoll in Eden Park. Its load-bearing concrete block walls are topped by sloping roofs finished in stainless steel. Inside, stainless steel walls glisten alongside exposed concrete block; the asymmetrical thrust stage boasts a choice of 24 entrance points. Supervising architects: Robert Habel-Hubert M. Garriot Associates. Engineers: Miller-

Tallarico-McNinch & Hoeffel (structural); Maxfield-Edwards-Backer & Associates (mechanical); Robert A. Hansen Assoc. (acoustical). Contractors: Turner Construction Co. HONORS: AISC Architectural Award of Excellence, 1969. SEE: Architectural Record (vol. 145) March 1969, 117-[128].

---

## HARRELL & HAMILTON

---

98.  2300 Riverside Apartments; Tulsa; OK; 1961. A 16-story luxury apartment tower which features continuous, six-foot wide balconies around its rectangular perimeter. Not only does almost every room have direct access to an outdoor space but the verandahs afford good sunshading and make interesting shadow patterns. Structural engineers: Hunt & Joiner. Landscape architects: Lambert Landscape Co. General contractor: Centex Construction Co. HONORS: AIA Merit Award, 1963. SEE: Architectural Forum (vol. 116) March 1962, [82]-[85].

---

## WALLACE K. HARRISON
Winner, AIA Gold Medal, 1967.

---

99.  Metropolitan Opera House, Lincoln Center; New York, NY; 1966. A grand manner home for a time-honored opera company. It combines fine acoustics and highly mechanized stage facilities with a modern baroque ambience rich in flowing lines, repeated curves, gilt, red plush and a grand staircase reminiscent of an elegant old European opera house. Planning and architectural liaison: Herman E. Krawitz. Acoustical consultants: Vilhelm L. Jordan and Cyril M. Harris. Engineers: Ammann & Whitney (structural); Syska & Hennessy (mechanical/electrical). General contractor: George A. Fuller Co. SEE: Architectural Record (vol. 140) September 1966, 149-160.

100.  United Nations Secretariat; New York, NY; 1950. This famous marble and glass slab of a building looms importantly over Manhattan's East River. It was designed by Harrison and Abramovitz in conjunction with an international "board of design," to provide office space for over 3500 UN employees plus living quarters for the Secretary General. Director of planning: Wallace K. Harrison; deputy director: Max Abramovitz. Associate architects: Gilmore D. Clarke, Louis Skidmore, Ralph Walker. Construction coordinator: James A. Dawson. Engineers: Syska & Hennessy (consulting engineers); Edwards & Hjorth (structural); Madigan-Hyland

(structural). Contractor: Fuller-Turner-Walsh-Slattery. HONORS: AIA Bicentennial List, 1 nomination. SEE: Architectural Forum (vol. 93) November 1950, [93]-[112].

## HARRISON & ABRAMOVITZ

101. ALCOA Building; Pittsburgh, PA; 1952. A 30-story office building innovatively sheathed in an Oxford gray, waffle-patterned aluminum skin. Other ALCOA-minded features built in were aluminum plumbing and wiring, and much of the original furniture boasted aluminum frames. Associate architects: Altenhof & Brown; Mitchell & Ritchey. Consultants: Edwards & Hjorth (structural); Jaros, Baum & Bolles (mechanical); Edward E. Ashley (electrical). General contractor: George A. Fuller Co. SEE: Architectural Forum (vol. 99) November 1953, 124-131.

102. First Presbyterian Church; Stamford, CT; 1958. A fish-shaped church on a grassy suburban site. Its arresting sanctuary is enclosed by a patchwork of zigzagging panels of concrete set with much colored bottle glass. Associated architects: Sherwood, Mills & Smith. Engineers: Edwards & Hjorth (structural); Fred S. Dubin Assoc. (mechanical/electrical). Consultants: Felix J. Samuely (structural); Bolt, Beranek & Newman (acoustical). Contractor: Deluca Construction Co. SEE: Architectural Forum (vol. 108) April 1958, 104-107.

103. Gov. Nelson A. Rockefeller Empire State Plaza; Albany, NY; 1978. This headquarters for New York State government, most often referred to as "the Albany Mall," also has been dubbed "Brasília North" and "the flat Acropolis." The complex, which was Gov. Rockefeller's brainchild, occupies almost 100 acres and includes ten monumental buildings sited on a five-level platform; total cost of its construction was over a billion dollars. Associated architects: James & Meadows & Howard (for Legislative Building); Carson, Lundin & Shaw (Swan Street Building); Sargent, Webster, Crenshaw & Folley (Justice Building). Engineers: Ammann & Whitney (structural); Syska & Hennessy (mechanical/electrical). Construction management: George A. Fuller Co. SEE: Architecture Plus (vol. 2) July-August 1974, [76]-[81]. Architectural Forum (vol. 136) May 1972, 7. Carol Krinsky, "St. Petersburg-on-the-Hudson: The Albany Mall," in Art, the Ape of Nature. New York: Abrams, 1981.

104. Illini Assembly Hall, University of Illinois; Urbana, IL; 1963 (Illus. 14). A 16,000-seat bowl for athletic, musical and theatrical events housed under a giant concrete dome with sinuously undulating lines. Its acoustics simulate outdoor conditions and its several

14.   Illini Assembly Hall, University of Illinois.   Harrison & Abramovitz.

interlocking systems of lighting can illuminate a variety of spectacles.  University architect:  Ernest L. Stouffer.  Engineers:
Ammann & Whitney (structural); Syska & Hennessy (mechanical/
electrical).  Acoustical consultants:  Bolt, Beranek & Newman.
Lighting consultant:  Lighting by Feder.  Site landscaping consultants:  Clarke & Rapuano.  General contractor:  Felmley-
Dickerson Co.  HONORS:  AIA Merit Award, 1964.  SEE:  Architectural Record (vol. 134) July 1963, 111-116.

105.   Interfaith Center, Brandeis University; Waltham, MA; 1955.   Three
separate chapels--Catholic, Jewish and Protestant--are grouped
harmoniously about a pool on a tree-fringed site.   Although their
designs vary, they are built of similar materials:  pale, glazed
brick with large areas of glass.  Engineers:  Eipel Engineering
(structural); Sears & Kopf (mechanical/electrical); Bolt, Beranek
& Newman (acoustical).  General contractor:  Lilly Construction
Co.  HONORS:  AIA Merit Award, 1956.  SEE:  Architectural
Record (vol. 116) September 1954, 9-11.  Architectural Record
(vol. 119) January 1956, 147-153.

106.   Phoenix Mutual Life Insurance Company Headquarters; Hartford, CT;
1964.   This office building is situated harmoniously alongside Constitution Plaza, designed by Charles DuBose (q. v. ).  It consists of
a 13-story elliptical tower set on a square, three-story pedestal.
Atop this supporting structure is a trim public plaza complete with

reflecting pool. SEE: Architectural Record (vol. 135) March 1964, 178-187. Interior Design (vol. 35) May 1964, 130-133+. Architect & Building News (vol. 229) January 12, 1966, 69-70.

---

## HARRISON, ABRAMOVITZ & ABBE

---

107. Corning Glass Center; Corning, NY; 1951. This popular showplace-- a long, low, glass and marble structure--comprises not only a working factory but also a museum exhibiting fine glass since ancient times, a library, and an area where visitors can view the manufacture of Steuben crystal. General contractor: George A. Fuller Construction Co. HONORS: AIA Merit Award, 1953. SEE: Architectural Forum (vol. 95) August 1951, 125-131.

108. U.S. Steel Building; Pittsburgh, PA; 1971. In this 64-story, triangular office tower--topped by a heliport for U.S. Steel executives-- weathering steel is used for most of the building's exposed parts. Other unusual structural features include the use of steel columns filled with a salt solution to provide the building with fireproof support and an unconventional pattern of wind bracing at every third floor. Partner in charge: Charles H. Abbe. Engineers: Skilling, Helle, Christianson & Robertson and Edwards & Hjorth (structural); Jaros, Baum & Bolles (mechanical). Landscape architects: Clarke & Rapuano. General contractor: Turner Construction Co. HONORS: AISC Architectural Award of Excellence, 1971. SEE: Architectural Forum (vol. 135) December 1971, [24]-29.

---

## HARTMAN-COX

---

109. Florence Hollis Hand Chapel, Mt. Vernon College; Washington, DC; 1970 (Illus. 15). This non-denominational chapel, sited on a steep slope, is built of red brick and slate and can be used for worship, musical performances or drama. Its boldly slanting, shed-like roof abounds in skylights and floods the interior with natural light. Engineers: James M. Cutts (structural); JEK Associates (mechanical/ electrical). Landscape architect: Lester A. Collins. General contractor: Edwin Davis. HONORS: AIA Honor Award, 1971; 1971 Community and Junior College Design Award. SEE: Architectural Forum (vol. 134) March 1971, [56]-[59].

15.  Florence Hollis Hand Chapel, Mt. Vernon College.  Hartman-Cox.
Photo: Y. Futagawa

JOHN HEJDUK

110. Foundation Building, Cooper Union; New York, NY; original building,
1858, renovation 1974. While the exterior of this Italianate landmark,
finished in stone with cast-iron detailing, was respectfully preserved,
its interior was gutted and completely rebuilt. The result: immaculate white spaces with refinement and grace to house Cooper Union's
School of Art and Architecture. SEE: Progressive Architecture (vol.
55) July 1974, 96-103. Progressive Architecture (vol. 56) July 1975,
50-57.

HELLMUTH, OBATA & KASSABAUM
Currently this firm is better known as HOK.

111. Chapel, Priory of St. Mary and St. Louis; near St. Louis, MO; 1962.
Three rings of thin-shell concrete parabolic arches shape this ex-
traordinary circular church. In its window areas, no glass is used.
Instead they are enclosed with two translucent plastic sheets: the
outer sheet a dark gray to contrast with the shell's white exterior,
the inner sheet white to glow with diffused natural light. Designer:
Gyo Obata. Supervising structural engineer: John P. Nix. Struc-
tural engineer: Paul Weidlinger. Mechanical engineer: Harold P.
Brehm. HONORS: PA Design Award, 1958. SEE: Architect &
Building News November 21, 1962, 753-756. Liturgical Arts (vol.
31) November 1962, 4-7, 12-25. Architectural Record (vol. 138)
August 1965, 144-145.

112. E. R. Squibb & Sons, Inc. Worldwide Headquarters; Lawrenceville,
NJ; 1972. This headquarters and research facility, set on gently
rolling acres, comprises seven brick and limestone buildings linked
by glassed-in walkways. Its handsomely designed interiors and
other amenities have won much praise; its 662-seat restaurant and
an art gallery look out over a man-made lake. Principal in charge
of design: Gyo Obata; principal in charge: Jerome J. Sincoff; interior designer: Michael Willis. Landscape architects: The Office
of Dan Kiley. Engineers: Le Messurier Assoc. (structural); Golder, Gass Associates (soils); Joseph R. Loring & Assoc. (mechani-
cal/electrical). Contractor: Huber, Hunt & Nichols. SEE: Architectural Record (vol. 153) June 1973, [139]-154.

113. National Air and Space Museum; Washington, DC; 1976 (Illus. 16). A
huge (685 x 225 feet) marble edifice designed to house such
twentieth-century wonders as Lindbergh's plane, the Spirit of St.
Louis, rockets, balloons, and the Apollo 11 moonship. It features
breathtaking interior spaces in which aircraft hang suspended from

16. National Air and Space Museum. Hellmuth, Obata & Kassabaum.
Photo: Y. Futagawa

exposed structural members. Principal in charge of design: Gyo Obata; principal in charge of project: Jerome Sincoff; project designer: Chih-Chen Jen. Consultants: Le Messurier Associates (structural); HOK Associates (mechanical/electrical/civil). Construction Manager: Gilbane Building Co. HONORS: AISC Architectural Award of Excellence, 1977. SEE: Progressive Architecture (vol. 57) July 1976, 70-75. AIA Journal (vol. 65) December 1965, 34-[37].

114. Neiman-Marcus Store, Galleria Post Oak; Houston, TX; 1968. A spectacular store in a spectacular shopping mall. The store's precast concrete exterior is accented by translucent onyx panels. Inside, escalators glide, glittering, through an open central well from which riders can see individualized shops all around. Principal in charge of design: Gyo Obata; project manager: Jon J. Worstell; project designer: Alvin Lever. Interior designer: Eleanor LeMaire Associates. Landscape architect: Sasaki, Dawson, DeMay Associates. Engineers: Elmer Ellisor Engineers (structural); Guerrero & McGuire and Leo L. Landauer & Associates (mechanical). Contractors: Henry C. Beck Co. and Linbeck Construction Corp. SEE: Architectural Record (vol. 146) July 1969, 135-[150]. Architectural Forum (vol. 136) April 1972, [24]-[39].

115. Pruitt-Igoe; St. Louis, MO; 1955. Probably the most notorious disaster in the field of public housing. When it opened, this complex of 30 eleven-story buildings was hailed for its imaginative design. For economy, elevators stopped only on the fourth, seventh and tenth floors; these floors featured sunny, 85-foot long galleries which were planned for use as indoor playgrounds and "neighborhood gathering places." Instead--in part due to changes in policies regarding tenants admitted--crime mounted and law-abiding tenants fled. In 1974, HUD demolished the project. Partner in charge of design: Minoru Yamasaki. Engineers: William C. E. Becker (structural); John D. Falvey (mechanical/electrical). SEE: Architectural Record (vol. 120) August 1956, 182-189. Architectural Forum (vol. 123) December 1965, 22-25. Building Official & Code Administrator (vol. 8) March 1974, 56-57.

116. St. Louis Planetarium; St. Louis, MO; 1963 (Illus. 17). This planetarium's 408-seat auditorium and dome are sheltered under a graceful parasol of a thin concrete shell. Around the dome, a spectators' ramp winds up to a skylighted penthouse--shielded from city lights by the shell's flaring rim--where stars can be observed directly. Partner in charge of design: Gyo Obata. Engineers: Albert Alper (structural); Harold P. Brehm (mechanical). Structural consultants: Ketchum, Konkel & Hastings. General contractor: Gamble Construction Co. HONORS: PA Design Citation, 1960. SEE: Architectural Forum (vol. 119) August 1963, [94]-[97].

17.  St. Louis Planetarium.  Hellmuth, Obata & Kassabaum.
     Photo:  Stephen Dunham, Kiku Obata

---

HELLMUTH, OBATA & KASSABAUM; BRODSKY, HOPF & ADLER

---

117.  Dallas/Fort Worth Regional Airport; near Dallas, TX; first phase,
      1973.  Conceived as a complex of 13 terminal units to be com-
      pleted by the year 2000, this airport's first four terminals, con-
      structed of beige concrete, were built as paired horseshoes each
      of which gives access to planes on the outside and parking for cars
      on the inside.  Principal in charge of design:  Gyo Obata.  Associ-
      ate architects:  Preston M. Geren, Jr.; Harrell & Hamilton.  En-
      gineers:  Le Messurier Associates and Terry-Rosenlund & Co.
      (structural); Herman Blum Consulting Engineers and Cowan, Love
      & Jackson (mechanical).  Landscape consultants:  Richard B. My-
      rick & Associates.  Construction management:  Parsons McKee.
      SEE:  Architectural Forum (vol. 136) May 1972, [24]-[31].  Con-
      crete (vol. 8) February 1974, 22-27.

HELLMUTH, YAMASAKI & LEINWEBER

118. Lambert-St. Louis Municipal Airport Terminal Building; St. Louis, MO; 1955. Intersecting barrel vaults shaped of thin-shell concrete frame a huge interior space: 412 feet long and 120 feet wide with window arches 32 feet high at the center. Plastic skylights set in long sweeping arcs supply additional natural light. Partner in charge of design: Minoru Yamasaki. Engineers: William C. E. Becker (structural); Ferris & Hamig (mechanical). Shell consultants: Roberts & Schaefer. Consultant during preliminaries: Edgardo Contini. HONORS: AIA Honor Award, 1956. SEE: Architectural Record (vol. 119) April 1956, 195-202, 278.

HERTZKA & KNOWLES; SKIDMORE, OWINGS & MERRILL

119. Crown Zellerbach Building; San Francisco, CA; 1959/1960. One of San Francisco's first glass-walled office towers, this 20-story building is set in an appealing and imaginative sunken garden. A surprisingly dainty one-story bank (S. O. M. 's Wells Fargo Bank, q. v.) is located at one corner of its plaza. Structural engineer: H. J. Brunnier. General contractor: Haas & Haynie. HONORS: AIA Merit Award, 1961. SEE: Architectural Record (vol. 125) April 1959, 163-174. Interiors (vol. 119) June 1960, 88-99. AIA Journal (vol. 35) April 1961, [87]. Japan Architect (vol. 36) April 1961, 64-69.

HODNE/STAGEBERG

120. 1199 Plaza Cooperative Housing; New York, NY; 1974 (Illus. 18). Sited on 12 acres in East Harlem this handsome, red brick-faced, middle income development provides 1,602,000 sq.ft. of residential space divided into 1590 desirable units. Each of its four buildings has a 31-story tower plus wings of from ten to six stories. Engineers: Robert Rosenwasser Associates (structural); Arthur L. Zigas & Associates (electrical/mechanical). Landscape architect: Herb Baldwin. Contractor: Starrett Brothers & Eken, Inc. HONORS: Bard Award, 1976; AIA Honor Award, 1977; Bartlett Award, 1977. SEE: Progressive Architecture (vol. 57) March 1976, 64-69.

18.  1199 Plaza Cooperative Housing.  Hodne, Stageberg.
Photo:  Norman McGrath

HOK  see  HELLMUTH, OBATA & KASSABAUM

FRANK L. HOPE

121.  San Diego Stadium; San Diego, CA; 1967.  The San Diego River was rerouted to put this 50,000-seat, baseball/football stadium safely above flood level.  Its strong, simple design gains added verve from the placement of its transportation facilities--corkscrew ramps and sleek elevator towers--as almost free-standing sculptural elements at its outer margins.  Principal in charge of architecture: Frank L. Hope Jr.; principal in charge of engineering:  Charles B. Hope; project designer:  R. Gary Allen.  Civil engineers:  City of San Diego.  Landscape architects:  Wimmer & Yamada.  General contractor:  Robertson-Larsen-Donovan.  HONORS:  AIA Honor Award, 1969; Bartlett Award, 1969.  SEE:  Progressive Architecture (vol. 48) December 1967, 98-101.  AIA Journal (vol. 51) June 1969, 95-[111].

MORTON HOPPENFELD, planner for THE ROUSE COMPANY

122.  Planned community: Columbia, MD.  An outstanding example of a successful "new town," a community planned and built from scratch. Plans for Columbia, located between Baltimore and Washington, D.C., stressed a heterogeneous mix of people, a lively downtown cultural center, and opportunities for employment nearby.  "New town zoning" was granted in 1965; by mid-1970, 3000 families were in residence and plans provided for 30,000 dwelling units by 1980. HONORS:  AIA Bicentennial List, 1 nomination.  SEE:  Architectural Forum (127) November 1967, 42-47.  Architects Yearbook (vol. 13) 1971, 34-47.

HOYLE, DORAN & BERRY  see  SERT, JACKSON & GOURLEY; HOYLE, DORAN & BERRY

## HUGH NEWELL JACOBSEN

123. Bolton Square; Baltimore, MD; 1967. This crisply attractive town-house complex, built on two inner-city blocks, creates an environment for elegant yet reasonably priced living. Positioned around a central oval, houses are dark burgundy brick with slate roofs and with all trim painted black. Each house also has a private, walled garden. Engineers: James Salmer; Carl Hansen. Contractor: Ames-Ennis Inc. HONORS: AIA Honor Award, 1969. SEE: Architectural Record (vol. 143) January 1968, [145]-160. AIA Journal (vol. 51) June 1969, 95-[111].

## CHARLES-EDOUARD JEANNERET-GRIS  see  LE CORBUSIER

## JOHN M. JOHANSEN

124. Charles Center Theater Building: The Morris Mechanic Theater; Baltimore, MD; 1967. On the outside it's knobby and roughly circular, modeled of muted golden poured-in-place concrete. Inside there's a clean-lined theater where a fan-shaped array of 1800 seats faces a stage with an extra wide (59 feet) proscenium opening. Associates in charge: Douglas Kingston, Jr. and Robert Kienker. Supervising architects: Cochran, Stephenson & Donkervoet. Engineers: Milo S. Ketchum & Partners (structural); Henry Adams Inc. (mechanical). Theater consultant: Jean Rosenthal. Acoustical consultant: Harold R. Mull. General contractor: Piracci Construction Co. SEE: Architectural Forum (vol. 126) May 1967, [72]-[79].

125. Mummers Theater: Oklahoma City, OK; 1970 (Illus. 19). This fiercely unconventional building--a jazzy assemblage of raw concrete, plain wooden decking and brightly painted steel ducts and towers--accommodates two shows at once. It contains both an arena theater (240 capacity) and a larger (592 capacity) thrust-stage theater. Associate in charge: Charles A. Ahlstrom. Supervising architects: Seminoff-Bowman-Bode. Engineers: Rudolph Besier (structural); John Altieri (mechanical/electrical). Landscape architect: Thomas Roberts. Stage designer: David Hays. General contractor: Harmon Construction Co. HONORS: AIA Honor Award, 1972. SEE: Architectural Forum (vol. 134) March 1971, 31-[37].

19. Mummers Theater. John M. Johansen.
    Photo: Balthazar Korab

126. Robert Hutchings Goddard Library, Clark University; Worcester, MA; 1968. Brick, concrete and lots of glass come together here in a library that is both functional and visually assertive. Unusual touches include Cubist-looking cantilevered outcroppings, "reading terraces," and lots of Johansen's characteristic bridges and ramps. Job captain: John Robie. Landscape architect: Corrier Anderson Guida. Engineers: Rudolph Besier (structural); John L. Altieri (mechanical). General contractor: Granger Contracting Co. HONORS: Award of Merit, Library Buildings 1970 Award Program, AIA, et al. SEE: Architectural Forum (vol. 131) September 1969, [40]-[47].

PHILIP JOHNSON
Winner, AIA Gold Medal, 1978. See also entry no. 182.

127. Amon Carter Museum of Western Art; Fort Worth, TX; 1961. A dignified, beautifully detailed museum faced with handcarved Texas shellstone and set on a multilevel plaza. Its spectacular main gallery is 24 feet high, 24 feet wide and 120 feet long. Supervising architect: Joseph R. Pelich. Engineers: Lev Zetlin (structural); Jaros, Baum & Bolles (mechanical). Interiors and landscaping: Philip Johnson. General contractor: Thomas S. Byrne, Inc. SEE: Architectural Forum (vol. 114) March 1961, 86-89.

128. Bailey Library, Hendrix College; Conway, AR; 1967. An unusual two story academic library, sited centrally on campus yet built almost completely underground so as to conserve open space. Ingenious landscaping, which includes many berms, transforms its roof area into a plaza and provides entry to the library from a connecting sunken plaza alongside. Associated architects: Wittenberg, Delony & Davidson, Inc. Engineers: W. H. Goodman, Jr. (mechanical); Engineering Consultants (structural). Landscape consultant: Joe Lambert. HONORS: Award of Merit, 1972 Library Buildings Award Program, AIA, et al. SEE: Architectural Record (vol. 146) December 1969, 87-96.

129. John F. Kennedy Memorial; Dallas, TX; 1970. A starkly simple, precast concrete structure which the architect has described as "a pair of magnets about to clamp together." It stands a few hundred yards from where President Kennedy was assassinated. Perspecta (vol. 11) 1967, 178-218. G. E. Kidder Smith, Pictorial History of Architecture in America. New York: American Heritage, 1976.

130. Kneses Tifereth Israel Synagogue; Port Chester, NY; 1956. A monumental building, white inside and out except where rows of slit windows, arrayed from floor to ceiling, are filled with brightly colored stained glass. As many as a thousand worshippers can be

seated in the combined sanctuary-social hall area, a giant room 37
feet high. Structural engineers: Eipel Engineering. Landscape
architect: Charles Middeleer. Contractor: Marcello Mezzullo.
SEE: Architectural Record (vol. 117) June 1955, 177-208. Architectural Record (vol. 120) December 1956, 123-129.

131. Munson-Williams-Proctor Institute; Utica, NY; 1960. A spacious,
granite-faced art museum with sharp, square lines and no windows
above the ground floor level. Giant bronze-sheathed girders, two
on each face, strike bluntly up the walls, then turn at right angles
to crisscross the roof. Unusual facilities inside include a children's
gallery and an auditorium that seats 300. Supervising architects:
Bice & Baird. Engineers: Lev Zetlin (structural); Fred S. Dubin
Associates (mechanical). Landscaping: Charles Middeleer. General contractor: George A. Fuller Co. SEE: Architectural Forum
(vol. 113) December 1960, 90-95.

132. Museum of Modern Art Additions and Sculpture Garden; New York,
NY; 1953; further changes and additions, 1964. The main museum
building, completed in 1939, was designed by Goodwin & Stone.
The added wing, distinguished by an ambience of tastefully appointed serenity, comprises classrooms and offices plus a small cafeteria which lets out upon the Abby Aldrich Rockefeller Sculpture
Garden. Associate architect: Landis Gores. Structural engineers:
Eipel Engineering Co. Landscape architect: James Fanning.
HONORS: Bard Award, 1966. SEE: Architectural Forum (vol.
102) May 1955, 146-149. Progressive Architecture (vol. 45) July
1964, 65-66.

133. Museum Wing for Pre-Columbian Art, Dumbarton Oaks; Washington,
DC; 1963. Each of this mini-museum's eight round, interconnect-
ing rooms, arranged in a tidy square around a central courtyard,
was designed to display the art of a different cultural group. Ex-
quisitely detailed, they feature curved glass walls, teak and marble floors, and eight separate domes linked together by a wavy-
margined, bronze-trimmed roof. Engineers: Lev Zetlin & Associates (structural); Jaros, Baum & Bolles (mechanical/electrical).
General contractor: George A. Fuller Co. SEE: Architectural
Forum (vol. 120) March 1964, 106-[111].

134. New York State Theater, Lincoln Center; New York, NY; 1964. The
lushly ornamented, red and gold interior of this 2700 seat theater
contrasts boldly with its neoclassic, travertine facade. Its three
balconies are horseshoe-shaped and, at the first balcony level, a
spectacular promenade area lures theatergoers at intermission.
Engineers: Severud-Elstad-Krueger Associates (structural); Syska
& Hennessy (mechanical). Consultants for theater architecture:
Ben Schlanger and Werner Gabler. Stage consultants: Donald
Oenslager and Walter Unruh. Contractor: Turner Construction
Co. SEE: Architectural Record (vol. 135) May 1964, 137-144.
Interiors (vol. 123) July 1964, [86]-91.

135. Sheldon Memorial Art Gallery, University of Nebraska; Lincoln, NE; 1963. This boldly elegant museum contains two floors of galleries, a 300-seat amphitheater, offices, and quarters for technical services. Its central Great Hall, 30 feet high, is glazed on both its outer walls. Most of the rest of the building is windowless, adorned by gracefully curving columns which trace a series of arches on its travertine exterior. Supervising architects: Hazen & Robinson. Engineers: Lev Zetlin & Associates (structural); Jaros, Baum & Bolles (mechanical). Contractor: Olson Construction Co. SEE: Architectural Record (vol. 134) August 1963, 129-131. Arts & Architecture (vol. 80) August 1963, 18-21, 30-31.

136. Shrine; New Harmony, IN; 1960. Built as a memorial to the Rappites who founded New Harmony as a utopian religious community in the early 1800's, the shrine is 50 feet high, with a cedar-shingled dome that undulates like a not quite fallen parachute. At its center, open to the air, rests a bronze "Virgin" sculpted by Jacques Lipschitz. Structural engineers: Wilcox & Erickson. General contractor: Traylor Brothers. HONORS: AIA Honor Award, 1961. SEE: Architectural Forum (vol. 111) September 1959, 115-123. Architectural Forum (vol. 113) September 1960, [128].

---

PHILIP JOHNSON/JOHN BURGEE

---

137. Boston Public Library Addition; Boston, MA; 1972. The library's original turn of the century building was designed in stately Renaissance Revival style by McKim, Mead & White. The boldly contrasting addition features giant exterior arches and columns that echo the older building's smaller, more conservative ones and a structural system that yields ample unobstructed space within. HONORS: AIA Bicentennial List, 4 nominations. SEE: Architectural Record (vol. 152) December 1972, 42. Progressive Architecture (vol. 54) February 1973, 32. George E. Kidder Smith, A Pictorial History of Architecture in America. New York: American Heritage, 1976.

138. IDS Center; Minneapolis, MN; 1972. Four buildings, including a 19-story hotel and the 51-story IDS tower, faced with mirror glass and strikingly notched, surround 20,000 square feet of covered mall. This central square, the Crystal Court, is canopied by an exhilaratingly varied grid of metal framed glass and plastic cubes and is penetrated by four Skyways (glassed-in, second floor level pedestrian walkways) that thread into it from adjoining streets. Associated architects: Edward F. Baker Associates. Engineers: Severud-Perrone-Sturn-Conlin-Bandel (structural); Cosentini Associates (mechanical). General contractors: Turner Construction Co. HONORS: AIA Honor Award, 1975; Bartlett Award, 1975;

AIA Bicentennial List, 1 nomination. SEE: Architectural Forum
(vol. 140) November 1973, 38-45. Johnson/Burgee: Architecture.
Text by Nory Miller. New York: Random House, 1979.

139. Pennzoil Place; Houston, TX; 1976. Here's 1,400,000 square feet of
office and commercial space wrapped in a dramatic package: twin
36-story trapezoidal towers which are mirror images of each other.
At ground level they define connected triangular plazas enclosed by
sloping walls of steel-framed glass. Joint architects: S. I. Mor-
ris Associates. Engineers: Ellisor Engineers (structural); I. A.
Namen & Associates (mechanical/electrical). Contractor: Zapata
Construction Corporation. HONORS: AIA Bicentennial List, 1
nomination; AIA Honor Award, 1977; AISC Architectural Award of
Excellence, 1977; R. S. Reynolds Memorial Award, 1977. SEE:
Architectural Record (vol. 160) November 1976, 101-110. Johnson/
Burgee: Architecture. Text by Nory Miller. Photographs by
Richard Payne. New York: Random House, 1979.

PHILIP JOHNSON and RICHARD FOSTER

140. Kline Science Center, Yale University; New Haven, CT; 1965. A
complex of buildings erected near Yale's older facilities for study
and research in the natural sciences, it provides added space for
work in biology, geology and chemistry as well as a related library.
The Kline Biology Tower, sited on a hill, is its most striking ele-
ment. Engineers: Lev Zetlin & Associates (structural); Strong &
Jones (mechanical). Landscape architects: Zion & Breen Associates. General contractor: E & P Construction Co. HONORS: PA
Design Award, 1964, for Kline Biology Tower; AIA Bicentennial
List, 1 nomination. SEE: Progressive Architecture (vol. 48) February 1967, [90]-97.

LOUIS I. KAHN
Winner, AIA Gold Medal 1971; Royal Gold Medal, 1972. See also entry
no. 209.

141. Alfred Newton Richards Medical Research Building, University of
Pennsylvania; Philadelphia, PA; 1960. Three 8-layered towers containing offices and labs cluster around a 10-story central tower
housing elevators, lavatories, pens for laboratory animals and similar "servant areas." Constructed of Kahn's customary reinforced
concrete but faced with brick to match the rest of the campus, the
building combines a look of "brawny sculpture" with efficient, pre-

cise design and economy of construction.  Structural consultant:
August E. Komendant.  Engineers:  Keast & Hood (structural);
Cronheim & Weger (mechanical).  Landscape architect:  Ian Mc-
Harg.  General contractor:  Joseph R. Farrell, Inc.  HONORS:
AIA Bicentennial List, 6 nominations.  SEE:  Architectural Forum
(vol. 113) July 1960, [82]-[87], 185.  Architectural Record (vol.
128) 149-156.  Y. Futagawa, ed., Louis I. Kahn:  Richards Medi-
cal Research Building ... Salk Institute....  Text by Fumihiko
Maki.  (Global Architecture, no. 5.)  Tokyo:  A. D. A. Edita, 1971.

142.  Center for British Art and Studies, Yale University; New Haven, CT;
1977 (Illus. 20).  Built of subtly detailed reinforced concrete and
located across the street from the Yale Art Gallery designed by
Kahn in association with Douglas Orr (q. v.), the center's strongly
rectilinear exterior is accentuated by dark glass and by panels of
gray stainless stell.  Its interior features include a cylindrical
stair enclosure, a three-story, skylight-roofed inner court, and
exposed satin-finish aluminum ducts.  Completed after Kahn's death
by Pellechia & Meyers, Architects.  Engineers:  Pfisterer, Tor &
Associates (structural); van Zelm, Heywood & Shadford (mechanical/
electrical).  General contractor:  George B. H. Macomber Co.
HONORS:  AIA Honor Award, 1978; Bartlett Award, 1978 (to Pellechia & Meyers).  SEE:  Architectural Record (vol. 161) June
1977, 95-104.

143.  Eleanor Donnelly Erdman Hall, Bryn Mawr College; Bryn Mawr, PA;
1965.  Dark gray slate outlined by white concrete forms the calmly
symmetrical facade of this dormitory/dining hall.  Its exterior design, marked by regular crenellations and set off by parapets,
calls to mind a medieval castle.  Structural consultant:  August E.
Komendant.  Engineers:  Keast & Hood (structural); John W. Fur-
low, Inc. (mechanical/electrical).  Landscape architect:  George
Patton.  General contractor:  Nason & Cullen.  SEE:  Architectural Forum (vol. 123) November 1965, [58]-[63].  Zodiac (vol. 17)
1967, [58]-[117].

144.  First Unitarian Church; Rochester, NY; 1967.  A church with the look
of a medieval fortress.  It is faced with red brick and includes
four towers whose unusual clerestory windows admit light from
above into the sanctuary.  HONORS:  AIA Bicentennial List, 2
nominations.  SEE:  Kokusai Kentiku (vol. 34) January 1967, 48-
50.  Architecture Canada (vol. 45) February 1968, 31-42.  G. E.
Kidder Smith, A Pictorial History of Architecture in America.
New York:  American Heritage, 1976.  Vol. 1, page 259.

145.  Kimbell Art Museum; Ft. Worth, TX; 1972.  A very large museum,
318 x 174 feet, constructed as a series of cycloid, post-tensioned

[Opposite:]  20.  Center for British Art and Studies, Yale University.
Louis I. Kahn.  Photo:  Henry Smith-Miller.

reinforced concrete vaults, each 100 x 22 feet and supported on four corner columns. Natural light flows in through skylights and lunettes; the exterior is enhanced by roofs of lead and infill walls of travertine. Project manager: Marshall D. Meyers. Resident associate architect: Preston M. Geren & Associates. Structural engineer: August E. Komendant. General contractor: Thos. S. Byrne & Co. Landscape architect: George Patton. HONORS: AIA Honor Award, 1975; Bartlett Award, 1975; AIA Bicentennial List, 3 nominations. SEE: Interiors (vol. 132) March 1973, 84-91; Architectural Review (vol. 155) June 1974, 319-329. Y. Futagawa, ed., Louis I. Kahn ... Kimbell Art Museum. Text by Marshall D. Meyers. (Global Architecture, no. 38.) Tokyo: A. D. A. Edita, 1976.

146. Phillips Exeter Academy Library; Exeter, NH; 1972. Brick, concrete and wood are masterfully combined in this large library for a private school. In its brick exterior, windows grow progressively larger from second to fifth levels while, at ground level, an arcade welcomes entry from the campus. Inside, the Great Hall features curving concrete stairs and, in powerfully trussed balcony walls, giant circular openings through which stack areas can be seen. Project manager: Winton F. Scott. Site manager: Earle W. Bolton. Engineers: Keast & Hood (structural); Dubin-Mindell-Bloome Associates (mechanical/electrical). Landscape architect: George Patton. Contractor: H. P. Cummings. HONORS: AIA Bicentennial List, 1 nomination. SEE: Architectural Forum (vol. 139) October 1973, [26]-[35]. Y. Fitagawa, ed., Louis I. Kahn ... Exeter Library, Phillips Exeter Academy.... Text by Romaldo Giurgola. (Global Architecture, no. 35.) Tokyo: A. D. A. Edita, 1975.

147. Salk Institute for Biological Studies; La Jolla, CA; 1965. A massive research complex built of elegantly finished reinforced concrete and sited on the shores of the Pacific. On either side of a garden stand two sternly sculptured laboratory buildings, each 65 feet wide and 245 feet long; individual "studies" for scientists are in towers facing onto the garden and open to sea breezes as well. Structural consultant: August E. Komendant. Associated structural engineers: Fervor-Dorland & Associates. Electrical-mechanical engineers: Fred F. Dubin Associates. Landscape architect: Roland S. Hoyt. SEE: Architectural Forum (vol. 122) May 1965, 36-45. Y. Futagawa, ed., Louis I. Kahn: Richards Medical Research Building ... Salk Institute.... Text by Fumihiko Maki. (Global Architecture, no. 5.) Tokyo: A. D. A. Edita, 1971.

---

KALLMAN, MCKINNELL & KNOWLES

---

148. Boston City Hall; Boston, MA; 1969. An extraordinary building like

a giant abstract sculpture, it won a design competition in 1962 but also has been compared to a bunker or an egg crate. It is set in City Hall Square--multi-leveled and brick paved--an exciting open space which reaches out to the Federal Office Building on one side and Faneuil Hall (see entry no. 341), down the hill, on the other. Associated architects: Campbell, Aldrich & Nulty. Project managers: Robert C. Abrahamson, Henry A. Wood. Design coordinator: Gordon F. Tully. Engineers: Le Messurier Associates (structural); Greenleaf Associates (mechanical). General contractor: J. W. Bateson Co., Inc. HONORS: AIA Honor Award, 1969; Bartlett Award, 1969; AIA Bicentennial List, 12 nominations. SEE: Architectural Forum (vol. 130) January-February 1969, 38-53. Architectural Record (vol. 145) February 1969, 133-144.

KELLY & GRUZEN
    Subsequent name of firm: GRUZEN & PARTNERS

149. Chatham Towers; New York, NY; 1965. Inexpensively built yet luxurious in feeling is this 240-unit, reinforced concrete, middle-income housing development in Lower Manhattan. Most apartments have corner exposures, many have terraces. Since the buildings take up just 15 percent of the site, there's room for a sophisticated plaza and a well-equipped playground. Associate in charge: George G. Shimamota; project architect: Raymond P. Tuccio. Engineers: Weinberger, Frieman, Leichtman & Quinn (structural); Herman Scherr (mechanical). Landscape architects: M. Paul Friedberg & Associates. HONORS: Award of Merit, 1964, New York State Architects Association; Bard Award, 1967. SEE: Progressive Architecture (vol. 47) February 1966, 132-139.

WILLIAM KESSLER

150. Center for Creative Studies, College of Art and Design; Detroit, MI; 1975. Built of precast concrete and featuring unusual cylindrical columns that are both striking and functional, here is an environment for design students that proudly reveals the bare facts about its structure. Modules repeat emphatically, most walls are left unpainted, and pipes are left exposed. Engineers: Robert Darvas & Associates (structural); Hoyem Associates (mechanical/electrical). Landscape architects: William Kessler & Associates. HONORS: AIA Honor Award, 1976; Bartlett Award, 1976. SEE: AIA Journal (vol. 65) April 1976, 36-57. Domus (no. 569) April 1977, 22-24.

## MORRIS KETCHUM, JR.

151.  Lila Acheson Wallace World of Birds Building, Bronx Zoo; New York, NY; 1972. Simulated natural environments for various types of birds are provided by "an asparagus-like bunch of cut-off cylinders, ellipses and free forms joined by ramps." Thanks to abundant sky-lights, natural vegetation thrives within. Job captain: Paul Palmieri. Engineers: Paul Weidlinger (structural); Wald & Zigas (mechanical/electrical). Contractor: William L. Crow Construction Co. HONORS: Bard Award, 1969. SEE: AIA Journal (vol. 58) August 1972, 53-54. Architectural Forum (vol. 137) September 1972, 62-65.

## KEYES, LETHBRIDGE & CONDON

152.  Tiber Island; Washington, DC; 1965. Built of reinforced concrete and gray-tan brick, this appealing residential complex near the Potomac River comprises four 8-story apartment buildings, 85 row houses with garden areas, a two-level parking garage, and a central plaza with a pool. Landscape architect: Eric Paepke. Engineers: Carl Hansen (structural); Kluckhuhn & McDavid Co. (mechanical); Eberlin & Eberlin (site). HONORS: AIA Honor Award, 1966. SEE: Architectural Forum (vol. 123) July-August 1965, [48]-51.

## KING & KING  see  I. M. PEI; KING & KING

## KISTNER, WRIGHT & WRIGHT; EDWARD H; FICKETT; S. B. BARNES

153.  Passenger-Cargo Terminal Berths 93A-93B; San Pedro, CA; 1963? A harbor terminal or "transit shed" for the loading and unloading of ships which innovatively provides separate facilities for the handling of passengers and of cargo. On the passenger level, there are lounges, customs inspection areas and a "spectators' waving gallery." Joint venture of Kistner, Wright & Wright and Edward H. Fickett, architects, and S. B. Barnes, structural engineer. Engineers: Los Angeles Harbor Department. Landscape architects: Armstrong & Sharfman. General contractor: L. C.

Dunn, Inc. HONORS: AISC Architectural Award of Excellence, 1963. SEE: Architectural Record (vol. 134) September 1963, 163-168. Arts and Architecture (vol. 80) August 1963, 26-27, 30.

---

VINCENT G. KLING
   Subsequent name of firm: THE KLING PARTNERSHIP

---

154. Municipal Services Building; Philadelphia, PA; 1965. A 16-story municipal office building largely elevated on columns above street level and sited atop a handsome plaza. Below street level, under the plaza, there's a huge public concourse where as many as 2000 people at a time can apply for licenses, pay bills to city bureaus, etc. Engineers: McCormick-Taylor Associates (structural); Charles S. Leopold, Inc. (mechanical/plumbing/electrical). HONORS: PA First Design Award, 1962; AIA Honor Award, 1967. SEE: Progressive Architecture (vol. 46) December 1965, 108-117, 151. AIA Journal (vol. 47) June 1967, 49.

155. Penn Center Transportation Building and Concourse; Philadelphia, PA; total Penn Center redevelopment, including City Hall West Plaza, completed 1976 (Illus. 21). Linked by a four-block underground concourse and shopping promenade, here subways, a railroad and intercity buses come together. Above ground there's a 1000-car parking garage, the Greyhound bus terminal and an 18-story office tower, the Transportation Building. Engineers: McCormick & Taylor Associates (structural); Robert J. Sigel, Inc. (mechanical/electrical). HONORS: PA Award Citation, 1955. SEE: Architectural Record (vol. 121) May 1957, 190-196.

156. Westinghouse Molecular Electronic Laboratory; Elkridge, MD; 1963. A facility designed with elaborate air conditioning and purification equipment to provide super-clean atmospheric conditions for the manufacture of tiny yet highly sophisticated electronic devices. Offices look out on a pleasant courtyard enhanced by a pool in which are stored 50,000 gallons of water needed for fire protection. Engineers: Allabach & Rennis (structural); Charles S. Leopold, Inc. (mechanical/electrical). General contractor: Kirby & McGuire. HONORS: AIA Merit Award, 1964; AISC Architectural Award of Excellence, 1964. SEE: Architectural Record (vol. 136) July 1964, 163-178. Progressive Architecture (vol. 45) November 1964, 158-160.

PENN CENTER CONCOURSE
PENN CENTRAL RAILROAD
Philadelphia, Pennsylvania
The Kling Partnership: Architects and Planners

21. Penn Center Transportation Building and Concourse. The Kling Partnership.

## CARL KOCH

157. Lewis Wharf Rehabilitation; Boston, MA; 1973. An attractive and popular complex of housing, offices, shops, restaurants and recreational facilities recycled from what formerly was a rundown waterfront area. Associates-in-charge: Margaret M. Ross, Leon Lipshutz. Engineers: Souza & True (structural); Shooshanian Engineering Associates (mechanical). Contractors: Kirkland Construc-

tion Co.   SEE: House and Home (vol. 45) February 1974, 88-93.
Architecture Plus (vol. 2) March-April 1974, 45-48.

---

ERNEST J. KUMP; MASTEN & HURD
   In 1970, Ernest J. Kump, Associates, won the AIA's Architectural
Firm Award.

---

158.   Foothill College; Los Altos Hills, CA; 1961.   Some forty buildings,
       on a 122-acre campus, all designed and built as a unit.   Though
       these buildings vary widely in size and purpose they were con-
       structed of the same materials (redwood, brick and concrete) and
       are sited tastefully to achieve a calm and gracious whole.   Engi-
       neers:  Huber & Knapik, Earl & Wright (structural); Keller & Gan-
       non (mechanical/electrical).   Landscape architects:  Sasaki, Walker
       & Associates.   General contractors:  Williams & Burrows; O. E.
       Anderson; Carl N. Swenson Co.   HONORS:  PA Design Citation,
       1960; AIA Honor Award, 1962; AIA Bicentennial List, 1 nomination.
       SEE:  Architectural Forum (vol. 116) February 1962, 52-[57].

---

LE CORBUSIER
   Winner, Royal Gold Medal, 1953; AIA Gold Medal, 1961.   His real
name was Charles-Edouard Jeanneret-Gris.

---

159.   Carpenter Center for the Visual Arts, Harvard University; Cambridge,
       MA; 1963.   This, Le Corbusier's only major building in the United
       States--designed to house classes in architecture, film and other
       arts--has struck some critics as surprisingly "modest and accom-
       modating."   Its concrete exterior has a smooth, precise finish; tall
       thin columns break up its interior spaces.   A great curvilinear
       ramp bisects the structure and connects with the main stair and an
       exhibition space.   Collaborating architects:  Sert, Jackson & Gour-
       ley.   Structural engineer:  William Le Messurier.   General con-
       tractor:  George A. Fuller Co.   HONORS:  AIA Bicentennial List--
       1 nomination.   SEE:  Architectural Record (vol. 133) April 1963,
       151-158.   Architectural Forum (vol. 119) October 1963, 104-107.
       Y. Futagawa, ed., Le Corbusier: Millowners Association Building
       ... Carpenter Center....  Text by Kenneth Frampton.   (Global
       Architecture, no. 37.)  Tokyo:  A.D.A. Edita, 1975.

22. St. Procopius Abbey Church and Monastery. Loebl Schlossman & Hackl. Photo: Balthazar Korab

LOEBL SCHLOSSMAN BENNETT & DART
Subsequent name of firm:  Loebl Schlossman & Hackl.

160.  St. Procopius Abbey Church and Monastery; Lisle, IL; 1972 (Illus.
      22).  Common brick, wood framing and concrete combined with
      originality and a strong sense of geometry provide living and work-
      ing quarters for a community of 100 Benedictine monks.  The ab-
      bey's centerpiece, a church that seats 700, has neither statuary
      nor stained glass nor elaborate altar; its ambience is one of "in-
      spired simplicity" conducive to meditation.  Partner in charge:
      Edward D. Dart.  Associate architect: Paul Straka.  Engineers:
      Eugene A. Dubin & Associates. (structural); William T. Brookman
      & Assoc. (Mechanical).  General contractor: McCarty Brothers,
      Inc.  HONORS: AIA Honor Award, 1973.  SEE: Architectural
      Forum (vol. 137) December 1972, [40]-45.  AIA Journal (vol. 59)
      May 1973, 42-43.

LOEBL, SCHLOSSMAN, BENNETT & DART; C. F. MURPHY ASSOCIATES

161.  Water Tower Place; Chicago, IL; 1976.  The base of this midtown com-
      plex contains a seven-level shopping mall with two department stores
      and over a hundred shops and other attractions centering around a
      Grand Atrium with a spectacular "cascading garden" escalator.  Above
      this base rises a tower with 44 floors of luxury condominiums and 22
      floors of hotel space.  Consulting architect: Warren Platner Asso-
      ciates.  SEE: Architectural Record (vol. 159) April 1976, [136]-
      [140].  Inland Architect (vol. 20) October 1976, 6-13.  Architec-
      tural Record (vol. 162) October 1977, 99-104.

EDUARDO LOPEZ  see  JORGE DEL RIO and EDUARDO LOPEZ

CHARLES LUCKMAN

162.  Prudential Center; Boston, MA; 1965.  Located on a spacious 31-acre
      site adjacent to downtown Boston, this complex comprises a 52-
      story office building, the Prudential Tower, for Prudential Insur-
      ance, the 29-story Sheraton-Boston Hotel and (linked to the hotel

by a covered bridge) the multi-purpose War Memorial Stadium. Overall planning: Charles Luckman Associates. Architects for Tower and Hotel: Charles Luckman Associates. Architects for Stadium: Hoyle, Doran & Berry. SEE: Architectural Record (vol. 135) March 1964, 190-191. Architectural Forum (vol. 122) May 1965, 24.

---

VICTOR A. LUNDY

---

163. Church of the Resurrection, East Harlem Protestant Parish; New York, NY; 1964. A small, inexpensively built but dramatically angled church surrounded by medium-rise public housing and, according to the architect, "designed as a piece of sculpture to be looked down upon from above." Engineers: Severud Associates (structural); Fred S. Dubin Assoc. (mechanical). General contractor: Thompson-Brinkworth, Inc. HONORS: AIA Merit Award, 1966. SEE: Architectural Forum (vol. 124) January 1966, 48-53.

164. Florida's Silver Springs; Silver Springs, FL; 1957. A complex of airy one- and two-story buildings serving a popular tourist resort that offers rides in glass-bottomed boats revealing wonders of underwater life. Included are a restaurant, a boat dock and a structure housing shops and offices that curves harmoniously along the banks of the Silver River. General contractor: John Rasmussen. HONORS: PA Award Citation, 1956; AIA Merit Award, 1959. SEE: Progressive Architecture (vol. 39) April 1958, 146-148.

165. Unitarian Meetinghouse; Hartford, CT; 1964. A ground-hugging church whose outline is defined by a circle of spiky reinforced concrete fins which support a system of concentric steel cables. Outside, roofs of heavy wooden decking span the spaces between the concrete fins while, inside, the central sanctuary boasts a remarkable ceiling that looks like a billowing web. SEE: Architectural Record (vol. 131) February 1962, 118-120. Architectural Forum (vol. 121) August-September 1964, 126-129. L'Architecture d'Aujourd'hui (vol. 35, no. 122) September 1965, 72-73.

166. Warm Mineral Springs Inn; Venice, FL; 1958. A one-story, L-shaped motel with a sprightly feeling all its own. Taller and shorter roofs--each a concrete shell on a stem, like a squared-off mushroom--alternate, checkerboard style. Inside, the checkerboard theme is repeated: ceilings over dining and sleeping areas are dark and low; over cooking and lounge areas, pale and high. Consulting engineers: Donald A. Sawyer (structural); Louis H. V. Smith (mechanical). General contractor: Spear, Inc. HONORS: PA Award Citation, 1958; AIA Merit Award, 1958. SEE: Architectural Forum (vol. 108) May 1958, 114-117.

MLTW/MOORE TURNBULL
      See also: MOORE, LYNDON, TURNBULL, WHITAKER, the firm from
which this one evolved.

167.  Faculty Club, University of California; Santa Barbara, CA; 1968 (Illus.
      23).  Standard components of a faculty club--dining facilities, guest
      rooms, meeting rooms and a swimming pool--plunked into a whim-
      sically theatrical setting complete with hanging neon lights, Pop Art
      graphics and other ostentatiously neo-roadhouse touches.  Partner
      in charge: Charles W. Moore.  Consulting architect: Thore H.
      Edgren.  Engineers: Davis & Moreau (structural); Archer-Spencer
      Engineering (mechanical).  General contractor: James I. Barnes
      Construction Co.  SEE: Architectural Forum (vol. 130) March
      1969, [78]-[85].

168.  Kresge College, University of California at Santa Cruz; Santa Cruz,
      CA; 1973.  A compact campus set among redwoods and modeled
      after a Mediterranean hillside village.  Its stuccoed woodframe
      buildings--painted white with accents of bright colors--are ar-
      ranged along a curving, 300-meter long "street" complete with a
      "triumphal arch" and a couple of plazas.  Principals in charge:
      Charles W. Moore, William Turnbull, Jr., Robert Simpson.  En-
      gineering consultants: Steve H. Sassoon & Assoc. (structural);
      Loran A. List (mechanical).  General contractor: Bogard Construc-
      tion, Inc.  HONORS: PA Design Citation, 1970.  SEE: Progres-
      sive Architecture (vol. 55) May 1974, 76-83.  Architectural Review
      (vol. 156) July 1974, 28-[42].  Process: Architecture (no. 3)
      1977, 135-149.

169.  Sea Ranch Swim and Tennis; Sonoma County, CA; 1967.  An amenity
      of the Sea Ranch Condominium (see entry no. 189) designed to
      blend into a sweep of rugged hills while shielding a pool and ten-
      nis court from chilly north winds.  A two-story unfinished redwood
      wall with attendant buttresses serves as a windbreak and sun re-
      flector.  Inside, white plywood walls sport boldly oversized multi-
      color graphics.  Structural engineers: Davis & Moreau and Gilbert,
      Forsberg, Diekmann & Schmidt.  Landscape architects: Lawrence
      Halprin & Assoc.  Graphic designer: Barbara Stauffacher.  Gen-
      eral contractor: Matthew Sylvia.  HONORS: PA Design Citation,
      1966; AIA Honor Award, 1968.  SEE: Zodiac (no. 17) 1967, 136-
      137.  AIA Journal (vol. 49) June 1968, 84-[104].  MLTW/Moore,
      Lyndon, Turnbull and Whitaker; The Sea Ranch ..., ed. and pho-
      tographed by Y. Futagawa.  Text by W. Turnbull, Jr. (Global Ar-
      chitecture, no. 3.)  Tokyo: A.D.A. Edita, 1970.

23. Faculty Club, University of California, Santa Barbara. MLTW.
Photo: © Morley Baer

24.  St. Francis Square.  Marquis & Stoller.
     Photo:  Karl Riek

GERALD McCUE
     Winner, Kemper Award, 1971

170. Research Laboratory D, Chevron Research Company; Richmond, CA; 1967. As part of a Standard Oil of California installation, this lab, equipped with an elaborate ventilation system, flaunts a phalanx of vertical exhaust flues on one long side and horizontal rows of air supply ducts on the other. Bluntly rectilinear, it is an economically built yet handsome example of "no-nonsense architecture." Engineers: John Blume & Assoc. (structural); Sanford Fox (mechanical). General contractor: Barrett Construction Co. HONORS: AIA Honor Award, 1968. SEE: Architectural Forum (vol. 124) April 1966, [40]-[47].

MANN & HARROVER

171. Memphis Metropolitan Airport; Memphis, TN; 1963. About a third of the passengers who use this busy inland airport have to change planes here. Arrival/departure gates are arranged efficiently along a Y-shaped concourse, the stem of which leads into the monumental central hall of the concrete-and-masonry terminal. Engineers: S. S. Kenworthy & Assoc. (structural); Allen & Hoshall (mechanical/electrical). Landscape architects: Ewald Associates. General contractor: J. A. Jones Construction Co. HONORS: PA Design Citation, 1961; AIA Merit Award, 1964. SEE: Architectural Record (vol. 134) October 1963, [165]-[172].

MARQUIS & STOLLER

172. St. Francis Square; San Francisco, CA; 1963 (Illus. 24). A low-rise development of 299 co-op apartments in an urban renewal area. Along with a YMCA, it occupies an attractively landscaped L-shaped megablock put together from three city blocks and the streets that used to divide them. Residents enjoy tree-lined walks and spacious recreational areas. Engineers: Eric Elsesser (structural); K. S. Oliphant (mechanical/electrical). Landscape architects: Lawrence Halprin & Assoc. General contractor: Jack Baskin. HONORS: AIA Merit Award, 1964; AIA Design Award for Nonprofit-Sponsored Low and Moderate Income Housing (1970). SEE: Arts and Architecture (vol. 81) August 1964, 14-16. L'Architecture d'Aujourd'hui (no. 120) April-May 1965, [77]-[79].

## RICHARD MEIER

173. Bronx Developmental Center; New York, NY; 1976 (Illus. 25). An arresting U-shaped complex, four stories high, this 384-bed residential and out-patient treatment center for the mentally retarded features small units where residents are trained to live outside in the community. Faced with aluminum panels and finished on the interior with a wide range of colors, it has been hailed as virtually "pure architecture"--but by the same token has been criticized for its perhaps inappropriately abstract, un-homelike quality. Architects: Richard Meier, Gerald Gurland, Sherman Kung, Henry Smith-Miller. Engineering consultants: Severud, Perrone, Sturm, Bandel (structural); Caretsky & Assoc. (mechanical). Landscape architects: Gangemi & De Bellis. HONORS: AIA Honor Award, 1977; Bard Award, 1977; Bartlett Award, 1977; 1977 Reynolds Memorial Award; AISC Architectural Award of Excellence, 1978. SEE: A + U (no. 64) April 1976, [96]-[115]. Progressive Architecture (vol. 58) July 1977, 43-54.

174. Twin Parks Northeast, The Bronx; New York, NY; 1972/1974. Tastefully designed limited-income housing ingeniously fitted into an irregular site on parts of three adjacent blocks. The 7-story and 16-story brick-faced concrete buildings frame sharply defined and handsomely detailed public spaces. Structural engineer: Robert Rosenwasser. Landscape architect: Joseph Gangemi. General contractor: Leon D. De Matteis & Sons. HONORS: Bard Award, 1973; AIA Honor Award, 1974. SEE: Architectural Forum (vol. 138) June 1973, 54-67. Architectural Record (vol. 154) July 1973, 89-98.

175. Westbeth Artists Housing; New York, NY; 1970. A stunning example of adaptive re-use: a block-square complex of eleven buildings formerly used by Bell Telephone rehabilitated and transformed into dramatically high-ceilinged yet moderately priced loft-style housing exclusively for artists. Provision was made for a communal gallery and other unusual amenities. Associates in charge: Murray Emslie, Gerald Gurland, Carl Meinhardt. Engineers: Felcher Atlas Associates (structural); Wald & Zigas (mechanical). General contractor: Graphic-Starrett Co. HONORS: AIA Design Award for Nonprofit-Sponsored Low and Moderate Income Housing (1970); AIA Honor Award, 1971. SEE: Architectural Record (vol. 147) March 1970, 103-106.

25. Bronx Developmental Center. Richard Meier. Photo: Ezra Stoller © Esto; courtesy of Reynolds Metals Company, Richmond, Va.

## ERICH MENDELSOHN

176.   Maimonides Health Center; San Francisco, CA; 1950.  As originally
       built, this hospital for the chronically ill had a light-hearted, tonic
       look largely due to blithely curving balconies with feathery white
       railings.  Unfortunately, modifications made some years later de-
       tracted from its airy charm.  Consulting engineer:  Isadore Thomp-
       son.  Contractor:  Barrett & Hilp.  SEE:  Architectural Forum
       (vol. 94) February 1951, 92-99.

177.   Mount Zion Temple and Center; St. Paul, MN; 1954.  This synagogue
       was completed after the architect's death in September 1953.  Its
       richly decorated interior hides behind a spartan facade and contains
       interesting symbolic touches such as ten ribbed sections, recalling
       the Ten Commandments, in both the chapel and sanctuary and
       twelve steps, representing the Twelve Tribes of Israel, rising to
       the ark.  Associate architect:  Michael Gallis.  Architects for
       completion:  Bergstedt & Hirsch.  Mechanical consultant:  Clyde E.
       Bentley.  Structural consultant:  Isadore Thompson.  General con-
       tractor:  Naugle-Leck.  SEE:  Architectural Forum (vol. 102) Feb-
       ruary 1955, 106-115.  L'Architecture d'Aujourd'hui (vol. 28) April-
       May 1957, 73-77.

## LUDWIG MIES VAN DER ROHE
Winner, AIA Gold Medal, 1960; Royal Gold Medal, 1959.

178.   Federal Center; Chicago, IL; overall plan and courthouse completed
       1964, remainder completed subsequently.  Less than half of the
       Center's one and a half block area in the heart of the Loop is
       taken up by its three buildings:  a 42-story office building, a 30-
       story office building/courthouse and a one-story, glass-walled post
       office, all marked by Mies's characteristic serenity of line and
       meticulous detailing.  Architects:  Chicago Federal Center Archi-
       tects, a joint venture of Schmidt Garden & Erikson, Ludwig Mies
       van der Rohe, C. F. Murphy Assoc. and A. Epstein & Son.
       HONORS:  AIA Bicentennial List, 1 nomination.  SEE:  Architec-
       tural Record (vol. 137) March 1965, 125-134.  G. E. Kidder
       Smith, A Pictorial History of Architecture in America.  New York:
       American Heritage, 1976.  Volume 2, page 520.

179.   Illinois Institute of Technology; Chicago, IL; various dates.  In 1939,
       Mies designed the entire campus but not all its buildings were ul-
       timately built to his design.  Those that are his display in common
       a regularly repeated standard unit, a steel framed structural bay

24 feet wide by 24 feet deep by 12 feet high. In 1956 Crown Hall was completed; Reyner Banham has called it "his masterpiece, the holy of holies, the architecture school." HONORS: AIA Bicentennial List, 6 nominations. SEE: Reyner Banham, Guide to Modern Architecture. London: Architectural Press, 1962. Y. Futagawa, ed., Mies van der Rohe: Crown Hall, ITT, Chicago.... Text by Ludwig Glaeser. (Global Architecture, no. 14.) Tokyo: A.D.A. Edita, 1972.

180. Lafayette Park; Detroit, MI; 1963. A residential complex on 78 acres, it comprises the 20-story Pavilion Apartments, a number of townhouses, and Lafayette Towers, a pair of 21-story apartment buildings each of which contains 300 units. Curtain walls here were among the first designed with sleeves for individual air conditioners. Engineers for Pavilion Apartments: Frank Kornacker (structural); William Goodman (mechanical/electrical). Engineers for Lafayette Towers: Nelson, Ostrom, Berman, Baskin & Assoc. (structural); William Goodman (mechanical/electrical). SEE: Architectural Record (vol. 127) April 1960, 170-173. Architectural Forum (vol. 119) September 1963, [80]-[91].

181. 860-880 Lake Shore Drive; Chicago, IL; 1951. Two clean lined, 26-story residential towers set at right angles to each other in a fashionable lakefront setting. Black-painted structural steel combines with floor-to-ceiling glass walls to create a "tower of glass" innovatively adapted to apartment living. Associated architects: Pace Associates; Holsman, Holsman, Klekamp & Taylor; Ludwig Mies van der Rohe. HONORS: AIA Bicentennial List, 5 nominations; Twenty-Five Year Award, American Institute of Architects, 1976. SEE: Architectural Forum (vol. 97) November 1952, 93-111.

## LUDWIG MIES VAN DER ROHE and PHILIP JOHNSON

182. Seagram Building; New York, NY; 1958. An office tower designed less for profit than to heighten the prestige of its namesake firm. Its sleek facade of bronze, travertine and tinted glass overlooks Park Avenue; it soars straight up for over 500 feet from a serene and spacious plaza paved with pink granite and inlaid with two symmetrical pools set with rows of fountains. Associate architects: Kahn & Jacobs. Engineers: Severud-Elstad-Kreuger (structural); Jaros, Baum & Bolles (mechanical). Landscape consultants: Karl Linn & Charles Middeleer. General contractor: George A. Fuller Co. HONORS: AIA Bicentennial List, 15 nominations. SEE: Architectural Forum (vol. 109) July 1958, 66-77.

## MILLER HANSON WESTERBECK BELL

183.   Butler Square; Minneapolis, MN; 1975.   Here's a huge landmark ware-
       house, occupying a full city block, which has been recycled into a
       multi-use center with retail shops and office space in one half and
       a hotel in the other.   Most of its original structural system of
       heavy Douglas fir columns and beams was retained and exposed.
       Collaborating project architect: Arvid Elness.   Structural engi-
       neers: Frank Horner.   TAC Engineering (electrical/plumbing).
       Contractor: Knutson Co.   HONORS: AIA Honor Award for Ex-
       tended Use, 1976.   SEE: Architectural Record (vol. 158) Decem-
       ber 1975, 108-112.

## MITCHELL/GIURGOLA
Winner of the AIA's Architectural Firm Award, 1976.

184.   Columbus East Senior High School; Columbus, IN; 1973.   This long,
       low-lying high school of over 2000 students has a crisp high-tech
       look about it.   Lots of aluminum panels and glass here and thought-
       ful energy efficient design--all set off by a whimsical triumphal
       arch.   Engineers: Keast & Hood (structural); Paul H. Yoemans,
       Inc. (mechanical/electrical); Geiger-Berger & Assoc. (air struc-
       ture).   Landscape architects: Clark & Rapuano.   Contractor:
       Geupel-Demares, Inc.   HONORS: AIA Honor Award, 1975.   SEE:
       A + U: Architecture and Urbanism (no. 12) 1975, 61-82.   Archi-
       tectural Record (vol. 159) April 1976, [107]-118.

185.   Penn Mutual Tower; Philadelphia, PA; 1975.   Located directly behind
       Independence Hall at a transition point between tall new buildings
       and more historic low ones, this 22-story office building has four
       differing facades, each keyed to harmonize amiably with its neigh-
       bors.   On one side, the four-story facade of an 1838 Egyptian Re-
       vival building has been erected as a freestanding sculptural wall that
       relates well to its vintage neighbors while it defines the Tower's
       entrance plaza.   Engineers: Skilling, Helle, Christiansen, Robert-
       son (structural); Robert J. Sigel, Inc. (mechanical/electrical).
       General contractor: Turner Construction Co.   HONORS: AIA Honor
       Award for Extended Use, 1977.   SEE: Progressive Architecture
       (vol. 57) April 1976, 72-75.   Process: Architecture (no. 2) Octo-
       ber 1977, 183-196.

## MITCHELL & RITCHEY

186. The Auditorium; Pittsburgh, PA; 1961. A huge circular arena, 417 feet in diameter, with a retractable dome--the first of its kind in the world. At the press of a button, it can open or close in 2 1/2 minutes. Consulting engineers: Ammann & Whitney. Engineers: Robert A. Zern (structural); Carl J. Long (electrical); Dzubay & Bedsole, John W. Mullin (mechanical). Landscape architects: Simonds & Simonds. General contractor: Dick Corporation. HONORS: PA Award Citation, 1954. SEE: Architectural Record (vol. 130) November 1961, [165]-[168].

## ARTHUR COTTON MOORE

187. Canal Square, Georgetown; Washington, DC; 1971 (Illus. 26). Shops, offices and restaurants enjoy a lively home in what formerly was a warehouse on the banks of a barge canal. Original timber columns, wood planking and exposed brick walls lend flavor to its renovated interiors; a contemporary addition in brick and glass helps enclose --and further spices--the square. Consultants: Cotton & Harris (mechanical); Milton Gurewitz (structural). HONORS: AIA Honor Award for Extended Use, 1977. SEE: Progressive Architecture (vol. 52) April 1971, 66-73.

188. Science Building, The Madeira School; Greenway, VA; 1976. The angular shape of this building at a private girls' school is largely determined by its solar collector roof. The collector is designed to provide 60 percent of the building's heat; in spring and fall it also heats an adjacent swimming pool. Consultants: James Madison Cutts (structural); Flack & Kurtz Consulting Engineers (mechanical/electrical). General contractor: Commercial Industrial Construction, Inc. HONORS: AIA Bicentennial List, 1 nomination. SEE: Progressive Architecture (vol. 57) February 1976, 54-57.

## MOORE, LYNDON, TURNBULL, WHITAKER; JOSEPH ESHERICK
See also MLTW/MOORE TURNBULL

189. Sea Ranch Condominium; Sonoma County, CA; 1966 (similar clusters of homes were added subsequently). A second-home community of wood-frame construction and largely unpainted, built along a wild,

26.  Canal Square.  Arthur Cotton Moore.
Photo:  Jim Berkon

windy and almost treeless stretch of the Pacific Coast.  The main
condominium building has ten ample rooms ranged around two courtyards.  In its lee nestle jagged, almost shed-like dwelling units,
each composed of a single great room imaginatively broken into
smaller areas by painted enclosures and lofts.  A group of less
unconventional homes on the huge property, formerly a sheep
ranch, were designed by Esherick.  Structural engineers:  Davis
& Morreau.  Landscape architects:  Lawrence Halprin & Assoc.
General contractor:  Matthew D. Sylvia.  HONORS:  PA Design
Citation, 1965; AIA Honor Award, 1967.  Special Citation, Homes
for Better Living Program, 1967, for house designed by Esherick.
SEE:  Progressive Architecture (vol. 47) May 1966, 120-137.
House & Home (vol. 32) September 1967, 90-101.  Charles Moore,
et al., The Place of Houses.  New York:  Holt, Rinehart & Win-
ston, 1974.  Y. Futagawa ed., MLTW/Moore, Lyndon, Turnbull &
Whitaker:  The Sea Ranch Condominium and Athletic Club #1 & #2.
Text by William Turnbull, Jr.  (Global Architecture Detail, no. 3.)
Tokyo:  A. D. A. Edita, 1976.

## LUIGI W. MORETTI

190. The Watergate; Washington, DC; 1965/1970. A waterfront complex of considerable distinction ... aside from its historic notoriety! Located on the Potomac, its five buildings--each significantly different from its neighbors--describe long free-form curves while their facades are marked irregularly with sweeping ranges of terraces. Included are 683 luxury apartments, offices, a hotel and a shopping center. Associated architects: Fischer-Elmore. SEE: Domus (vol. 419) October 1964, 1-[22]. Bauwelt (vol. 61, no. 16) April 20, 1970, 593-594.

## WILLIAM MORGAN

191. Pyramid Condominium; Ocean City; MD; 1975. The unusual V-shaped plan of this 20-story beachfront condo gives every apartment cross ventilation, a terrace and an ocean view. From the front, its striking geometric lines suggest a pyramid. Project manager: Thomas A. McCrary. Project architect: Theodore C. Strader. Consultants: Sherrer-Bauman & Assoc. (structural); Geiger-Berger Associates (special structural); Archison & Keller (mechanical). HONORS: PA Design Citation, 1975. SEE: Progressive Architecture (vol. 57) September 1976, 64-67. A + U: Architecture and Urbanism (no. 82) September 1977, [37]-[48].

## WILLIAM C. MUCHOW
See also ARCHITECTURAL ASSOCIATES COLORADO

192. First Federal Savings and Loan Association of Denver; Denver, CO; 1954. A small local bank that uses simple lines, lots of glass and custom designed furnishings to create a sense of spaciousness. Engineers: Ketchum & Konkel (structural); M. S. Wilson (mechanical). General contractor: Olson & Hart. HONORS: PA Award Citation, 1954; AIA Merit Award, 1954. SEE: Progressive Architecture (vol. 36) September 1955, 110-113.

27.  Park Central.  W. C. Muchow Associates.

## MUCHOW ASSOCIATES

193.  Park Central; Denver, CO; 1974 (Illus. 27).  A downtown banking/
shopping/office/garage complex that pulls together into one unified
whole elements of varying heights and depths.  Local authorities
had imposed different height limitations on different parts of the
site; this megastructure's disparate elements gain unity from its
striking dark exterior of black anodized aluminum and solar bronze
glass and from the skillful balancing of its masses.  Project designer: George Hoover.  Engineers: Ketchum, Konkel, Barrett,
Nickel, Austin (structural); Hadji & Associates (mechanical/elec-
trical).  Landscape architect: Chris Moritz.  General contractor:
C. H. Leavell & Co.  HONORS: AIA Honor Award, 1975; Bartlett
Award, 1975.  SEE: Architectural Record (vol. 155) April 1974,
107-112.  AIA Journal (vol. 63) May 1975, 26-43.

C. F. MURPHY ASSOCIATES
Subsequent name of firm: MURPHY/JAHN. See also entry no. 161.

194. Auraria Learning Resources Center; Denver, CO; 1976. Aluminum sun screens on two sides work together with floor to ceiling glass to make the most of Denver's sunny climate for this two-story library and media center shared by Denver Community College, Metropolitan State College and the University of Colorado. Inside are 184,000 square feet of flexible loft space without ceilings; structural, mechanical and electrical systems are left exposed overhead. Partner in charge: Helmut Jahn; project architect: David Hovey. Engineers: Zeller & Grey (structural); C. F. Murphy Associates (mechanical/electrical). General contractor: Martin K. Eby Construction Co. HONORS: Chicago AIA Distinguished Building Award, 1976. SEE: Architectural Record (vol. 162) November 1977, 109-124. A + U: Architecture and Urbanism (no. 10) October 1978, 55-62.

195. Crosby Kemper Memorial Arena; Kansas City, MO; 1974. This multi-purpose indoor arena seats 16,000-18,000 people for sports events, theatrical spectacles and conventions. Its enclosure, clad in metal panels, is dramatically framed by three gigantic exposed roof trusses, meticulously scaled and detailed. Partner in charge: Helmut Jahn; project architect: James Goettsch. Landscape architects: Parks and Recreation, Kansas City. Acoustical consultants: Coffeen, Gatley & Assoc. Contractor: J. E. Dunn Construction Co. HONORS: AISC Architectural Award of Excellence, 1975; AIA Honor Award, 1976; Bartlett Award, 1976. SEE: Architectural Record (vol. 159) March 1976, [109]-[114]. AIA Journal (vol. 65) April 1976, 36-57.

196. McCormick Place-On-The-Lake; Chicago, IL; 1970. A huge, glass-walled convention center on the banks of Lake Michigan, built to replace the McCormick Place complex destroyed by fire in 1967. Its two companion structures--one housing a 4451-seat theater plus restaurants and meeting rooms, the other providing over 300,000 square feet of exhibition space--share a single, dramatically steel-trussed roof. Engineers: C. F. Murphy Associates. Consultants: John W. Ditamore (theater); Bolt, Beranek & Newman (acoustics). General contractors: Gust K. Newberg Construction and Paschen Contractors (joint venture). HONORS: AIA Honor Award, 1972; AISC Architectural Award of Excellence, 1972; Bartlett Award, 1972. SEE: Architectural Record (vol. 149) May 1971, 95-106. Architectural Forum (vol. 135) November 1971, 36-57.

197. O'Hare International Airport, Chicago, IL; 1963 plus additions completed 1973. The C. F. Murphy firm inherited an existing runway, control tower and partly finished terminal built according to an

earlier plan; then they had to negotiate with the 13 airlines and arrive at a compromise design. A striking circular restaurant building with a skylighted central hall is one of the most appealing elements of this sprawling, often modified airport. Partner in charge: Carter H. Manny, Jr. SEE: Architectural Record (vol. 152) October 1972, 127-142. Inland Architect (vol. 17) August 1973, 18-22.

198. Richard J. Daley Center (formerly Chicago Civic Center); Chicago, IL; 1966 (Illus. 28). A 648-foot-high tower set on a two and a half acre plaza and designed to house offices and courtrooms. Faced with oxidizing steel and glass, its structure is daring. There are no major interior columns, just twelve huge cruciform exterior columns with 87-foot steel trusses running lengthwise and 48-foot spans running crosswise. Associate architects: Skidmore, Owings & Merrill and Loebl, Schlossman, Bennett & Dart. Consulting engineers: Severud-Elstad-Kreuger Associates (structural). General contractor: Gust K. Newberg Construction Co. HONORS: AISC Architectural Award of Excellence, 1966; AIA Honor Award, 1968; AIA Bicentennial List, 1 nomination. SEE: Architectural Forum (vol. 125) October 1966, [33]-[37]. Casabella (no. 309) September 1966, 48-55.

199. St. Mary's Athletic Facility, St. Mary's College; Notre Dame, IN; 1977. A stripped down, colorful, high-tech gymnasium that matches the high spirits of athletes at this small women's college. Fiberglass used in translucent wall panels and in transparent, curved clerestory windows combine with exposed red trusses, blue pipes and yellow ducts to fashion its light and lively good looks. Design principal: Helmut Jahn; project architect: James Goettsch. General contractor: The Hickey Co. HONORS: Chicago AIA Distinguished Building Award, 1977; AISC Architectural Award of Excellence, 1978. SEE: Progressive Architecture (vol. 59) July 1978, 58-61.

## MURPHY & MACKEY

200. Climatron, Botanical Garden; St. Louis, MO; 1960. A climate controlled greenhouse topped by a giant, aluminum-framed geodesic dome. A range of climates can be simulated at the same time, unusual displays such as a waterfall and a bog can be presented and, at night, dramatic illumination sets the dome glowing like an incandescent globe. Dome consultant: Synergetics, Inc. Mechanical engineer: Paul Londe. HONORS: R. S. Reynolds Memorial Award, 1961; AIA Bicentennial List, 1 nomination. SEE: AIA Journal (vol. 35) May 1961, 27-32. Progressive Architecture (vol. 42) April 1961, 174-178.

28. Richard J. Daley Center. C. F. Murphy Associates.
Photo: Hedrich-Blessing

## MYERS & BENNETT

201. East Bank Bookstore/Admissions and Records Facility (Williamson Hall), University of Minnesota; Minneapolis, MN; 1977. All but 5 percent of this highly energy-efficient, cast-in-place concrete, mixed-occupancy building is underground; yet, thanks to clerestory windows and an interior courtyard, it's a bright and cheerful place. Engineers: Meyer, Borgman & Johnson, Inc. (structural); Oftedal, Locke, Broadston & Assoc. (mechanical/electrical). General contractor: Lovering Associates. HONORS: PA Design Award, 1975; Merit Award, Minnesota AIA, 1977. SEE: Architecture Minnesota (vol. 3) November-December 1977, 19-27. AIA Journal (vol. 67) April 1978, 34-[51].

## NARAMORE, BAIN, BRADY & JOHANSON

202. Seattle-First National Bank; Seattle, WA; 1969. This 50-story office tower, sheathed in bronze anodized aluminum, was erected on a very steep site; downhill it has four more levels than on its uphill side! Uphill there's a gracious plaza with trees and sculpture. Unusual and attractive public banking facilities, located partly below grade, are reached by escalator from the Plaza lobby. Partner in charge: Perry B. Johanson. Project architect: Robert J. Pope; project designer: Donald A. Winkelmann. Engineers: Skilling, Helle, Christiansen, Robertson (structural); Valentine, Fisher & Tomlinson (mechanical/electrical). Consultant: Pietro Belluschi. Landscape architect: William Teufel. Contractor: Howard S. Wright Construction Co. HONORS: AISC Architectural Award of Excellence, 1969. SEE: Architectural Record (vol. 147) June 1970, 129-136.

## RICHARD J. NEUTRA
Winner, AIA Gold Medal, 1977 (awarded posthumously)

203. Eagle Rock Playground Club House; Los Angeles, CA; 1953. A low rectangular clubhouse, set in a public park, that offers open air pavilion spaces on three sides. A raised rectangular platform at one end reaches out over a reflecting pool to a hillside slope to make the most of a natural amphitheater. Collaborators: Dion Neutra and John Blanton. HONORS: AIA Merit Award, 1955.

SEE: <u>Arts and Architecture</u> (vol. 73) April 1956, 14-15. <u>Architectural Record</u> (vol. 121) March 1957, 213-216.

204. Northwestern Mutual Fire Association Building; Los Angeles, CA; 1951. A small office building with strong, simple lines, built of brick, steel, aluminum and glass. Vertical louvers on the outside and "egg-crate" ceilings on the inside provide decoration while they lessen glare. Contractor: C. W. Driver. HONORS: AIA Merit Award, 1952. SEE: <u>Architectural Forum</u> (vol. 96) 111-113. <u>Architectural Review</u> (vol. 112) October 1952, 227-234.

## MATTHEW NOWICKI

205. Dorton Arena; Raleigh, NC; 1953. Grandly sweeping lines and bold engineering characterize this stadium--officially known as the North Carolina State Fair Livestock Judging Pavilion, though more familiarly called the Cow Palace. Its dramatic outline is determined by two huge interlocking parabolic arches which rise obliquely to a height of 90 feet above the ground; almost 10,000 people can be seated within it. Architect for completion after Nowicki's death in 1950: William Henley Deitrick. Consulting engineers: Severud, Elstad & Krueger. General contractor: William Muirhead Construction Co. HONORS: AIA Honor Award, 1953. SEE: <u>Architectural Forum</u> (vol. 97) October 1952, 134-139. <u>Architectural Forum</u> (vol. 100) April 1954, 130-134.

## A. G. O'DELL, JR.

206. Auditorium and Coliseum, Civic Center; Charlotte, NC; 1956. Sharing parking space and a plaza on a 23-acre site are a 2500-seat auditorium for concerts and theatrical presentations and a round coliseum that seats 13,500 for sports events and other spectacles. Their construction is of concrete and steel with the coliseum dome covered in aluminum. Consulting engineers: Severud-Elstad-Krueger (structural); W. P. Wells (mechanical). Acoustical consultants: Bolt, Beranek & Newman. Landscape architect: John Lippard. General contractor: Thompson & Street. SEE: <u>Progressive Architecture</u> (vol. 36) June 1955, 134-135. <u>Progressive Architecture</u> (vol. 37) September 1956, 112-121.

## ODELL ASSOCIATES

207.  Blue Cross and Blue Shield of North Carolina Service Center; Chapel
      Hill, NC; 1973.  The reflective glass walls of this regional head-
      quarters slope sharply to give it a dynamic-looking rhomboid shape.
      One practical by-product:  since these walls roughly parallel the
      rays of the sun, direct heat gain is considerably lower than it
      would be for a vertical, glass-enclosed building.  General contrac-
      tor: Nello L. Teer Company.  HONORS: AISC Architectural
      Award of Excellence, 1975.  SEE: Architectural Review (vol. 155)
      April 1974, 242.  Architectural Record (vol. 155) May 1974, 133-
      140.

208.  Burlington Corporate Headquarters; Greensboro, NC; 1971.  Sited on
      a lushly landscaped 34-acre former estate--complete with pool, high
      spouting fountain and an intriguing sculpture--this corporate head-
      quarters complex comprises two structures joined by bridges at
      three points.  Its six-story office structure is walled in reflecting
      glass and enclosed in a striking framework of exposed steel truss-
      es.  General contractor: Daniel Construction Company.  HONORS:
      AISC Architectural Award of Excellence, 1971.  SEE: Architectur-
      al Record (vol. 151) February 1972, [113]-[128].

DONALD OLSEN  see  JOSEPH ESHERICK; DONALD OLSEN; VERNON
      DEMARS

## DOUGLAS ORR and LOUIS KAHN

209.  Yale University Art Gallery and Design Center; New Haven, CT; 1953.
      This reinforced concrete building, designed to provide virtually un-
      broken loft space to be partitioned at will for changing exhibits, has
      been widely praised for its candid yet beautifully detailed exposure
      of its structural elements.  As one critic put it, "here structure is
      so integral with architecture it has acquired the value of ornament."
      Engineers: Henry A. Pfisterer (structural); Meyer, Strong & Jones
      (mechanical).  Landscape consultant: Christopher Tunnard.  Gener-
      al contractor: George B. H. Macomber Co.  HONORS: AIA Bicen-
      tennial List, 2 nominations.  SEE: Progressive Architecture (vol.
      35) May 1954, 88-101, 130-131.

JOHN B. PARKIN ASSOCIATES  see  VILJO REVELL; JOHN B. PARKIN
   ASSOCIATES

I. M. PEI
   In 1968, I. M. Pei & Partners won the AIA's Architectural Firm
Award.

210.   Denver Hilton Hotel; Denver, CO; 1960.  Sited on fashionable Zeck-
       endorf Plaza, this 21-story, 884-room hotel features a geometrically
       patterned curtain wall of red granite aggregate and numerous spec-
       tacular interior spaces including a block-long gold ceilinged lobby
       and a bridge, enclosed in arching plastic, which connects the lobby
       and a department store.  Partner in charge: Eason Leonard; in
       charge of design: Araldo Cossuta.  Associated architects: Rogers
       & Butler.  Consultant: William R. Tabler.  Engineers: Weiskopf
       & Pickworth (structural); Jaros, Baum & Bolles (mechanical/elec-
       trical).  General contractor: Webb & Knapp.  HONORS: AIA Merit
       Award, 1961.  SEE: Architectural Forum (vol. 113) August 1960,
       94-99.  Interiors (vol. 119) October 1960, 109-117.

211.   Des Moines Art Center Addition; Des Moines, IA; 1968.  The original
       museum building was designed by Eliel Saarinen and completed in
       1948.  Pei's harmonious addition, a sculpture wing, encloses the
       fourth side of a central courtyard; its skylights and expanses of
       deeply recessed windows serve to bathe the sculpture in natural
       light.  Architects in charge: Richards M. Mixon and Graeme A.
       Whitelaw.  Engineers: Weiskopf & Pickworth (structural); Robson
       & Woese (mechanical/electrical).  General contractor: The Weitz
       Co.  HONORS: AIA Honor Award, 1969.  SEE: Architectural
       Forum (vol. 130) June 1969, 54-[67].

212.   East Building, National Gallery of Art; Washington, DC; 1978.  This
       marble, glass and concrete addition to a time-honored neoclassical
       gallery is confidently contemporary.  Its lines are sleekly geomet-
       ric; triangles recur in its plan and detailing; and exciting interior
       spaces abound.  Engineers: Weiskopf & Pickworth (structural);
       Syska & Hennessy (mechanical/electrical).  Landscape architects:
       Kiley, Tyndall, Walker.  Construction manager: Carl Morse,
       Morse/Diesel, Inc.  Builder: Charles H. Tomkins Co.  HONORS:
       AIA Bicentennial List, 1 nomination.  SEE: Architectural Record
       (vol. 164) August 1978, 79-92 and cover.

213.   88 Pine Street; New York, NY; 1973.  This 33-story, Wall Street
       area office building with a river view stands out thanks to startling
       white curtain walls made of aluminum with a baked-on enamel

29. Everson Museum of Art. I. M. Pei.
Photo: © 1969 Ezra Stoller (Esto)

coating. Its elevator core is set off-center to provide large "bull-pen" areas on one side, space for small private offices on the other. Associate partner in charge: James Ingo Freed. Engineers: The Office of James Ruderman (structural); Cosentini Associates (mechanical/electrical). HONORS: R. S. Reynolds Memorial Award, 1974; AIA Honor Award, 1975. SEE: <u>Architectural Record</u> (vol. 157) April 1975, 123-128.

214. Everson Museum of Art; Syracuse, NY; 1968 (Illus. 29). This small museum built of concrete in an urban renewal area has coolly abstract lines inside and out. Its square-cut upper floors cantilever far out over a plaza; inside there's a sinuous spiral staircase and a two-level, skylit sculpture court. Project associate: Kellogg Wong. Associate architects: Pederson, Hueber, Hares & Glavin. Engineers: R. R. Nicolet & Assoc. (structural); Robson & Woese Inc. (mechanical). General contractor: William C. Pahl Construc-

tion Co.   HONORS:  AIA Honor Award, 1969; AIA Bicentennial List, 1 nomination.  SEE:  Architectural Forum (vol. 130) June 1969, 54-[67].

215.   Herbert F. Johnson Museum of Art, Cornell University; Ithaca, NY; 1973.   A concrete tower with assertive, abstract lines set on a promontory that overlooks a scenic lake and forms one end of a quadrangle otherwise bordered by quietly traditional low stone buildings.   Two floors above grade, an open air sculpture court occupies a multi-story space that is lidded by a floor of galleries and lounges.   Architect in charge: John L. Sullivan III.   Engineers:  Nicolet Dressel Mercille, Ltd. (structural); Segner & Dalton (mechanical).   Landscape architects:  Dan Kiley & Partners.   General contractor:  William C. Pahl Construction Co.   HONORS:  AIA Honor Award, 1975.   SEE:  Architecture Plus (vol. 2) January/February 1974, [52]-[59].

216.   John Hancock Tower; Boston, MA; 1975.   This 60-story office building, sheathed in reflective glass, has been roundly praised for fitting 2,000,000 square feet of space into a small site while consorting agreeably with landmarks on an historic square.   But when its glass panes started breaking by the dozens, lawsuits proliferated and a drastic program of reglazing had to be initiated.   Design partner:  Harry N. Cobb.   Engineers:  The Office of James Ruderman (structural); Cosentini Associates (mechanical/electrical).   Contractor:  Gilbane Building Company.   HONORS:  AIA Bicentennial List, 2 nominations; AIA Honor Award, 1977; AISC Architectural Award of Excellence, 1977.   SEE:  AIA Journal (vol. 66) May 1977, 37.   Architectural Record (vol. 161) June 1977, 117-126.

217.   Mile High Center; Denver, CO; 1955.   A 23-story office tower faced with an interweaving pattern of dark gray anodized aluminum and buff porcelain-enameled steel.   There's a freestanding black steel entrance canopy and, behind the main lobby, a colonnade walk that looks out on two fountain-pools.   Associated architects:  Kahn & Jacobs; G. Meredith Musick.   Consulting engineers:  Jaros, Baum & Bolles; Severud-Elstad-Krueger.   General contractor:  George A. Fuller Co.   HONORS:  AIA Merit Award, 1959.   SEE:  Architectural Forum (vol. 103) November 1955, 128-137.

218.   National Center for Atmospheric Research; near Boulder, CO; 1967.   This sharply angular and irregularly shaped cluster of research facilities, set against a background of rugged mountains, was inspired by the cliff dwellings of pre-Columbian Indians.   Here are towers, battlements and parapets--all modeled out of bush-hammered pinkish concrete.   Associates in charge:  James P. Morris, Richards Mixon, Robert Lym.   Engineers:  Weiskopf & Pickworth (structural); Jaros Baum & Bolles (mechanical).   Landscape architect:  Dan Kiley.   General contractor:  Martin K. Eby Construction Co.   HONORS:  AIA Bicentennial List, 1 nomination.   SEE:  Architectural Forum (vol. 127) October 1967, 145-154.   Y. Futagawa, ed.,

I. M. Pei & Partners: National Center for Atmospheric Research
.... Text by William Marlin. (Global Architecture, no. 41.)
Tokyo: A. D. A. Edita, 1976.

219. Paul Mellon Center for the Arts, Choate School and Rosemary Hall;
Wallingford, CT; 1972. Shared by two prep schools and housing a
theater, studios, classrooms and a lounge, this concrete-and-steel,
frankly asymmetrical center boasts exciting interior spaces and a
strong sense of interplay between indoors and outdoors. Its two
component structures are linked by a square cut bridge under which
runs a tile paved pathway that links the two schools. Architect in
charge: Ralph Heisel. Engineers: Olaf Soot (structural); Campbell & Friedland (mechanical). Theater consultants: George Izenour
Associates. Landscape architect: Joseph R. Gangemi. General
contractor: George B. H. Macomber Co. HONORS: AIA Honor
Award, 1974. SEE: Architectural Record (vol. 153) January 1973,
[111]-118.

220. Society Hill Apartments; Philadelphia, PA; townhouses completed
1963, Society Hill Towers 1964. Here's urban redevelopment with
understated good taste. Three-story brick townhouses, arranged
around a courtyard, share long continuous walls broken only by
windows and arched private entrances; their companion 31-story
apartment buildings are serenely simple concrete and glass slabs.
Job captain for townhouses: Owren J. Aftreth. Associate architects for townhouses: Wright, Andrade & Amenta & Gane. General contractor for townhouses: Jack Feldman. SEE: Architectural Forum (vol. 118) April 1963, 90. Progressive Architecture
(vol. 45) December 1964, 188-191.

221. University Plaza, Greenwich Village; New York, NY; 1966 (Illus. 30).
Three almost identical 30-story apartment slabs arranged in pinwheel fashion on a spacious landscaped site and designed to serve
as housing for New York University faculty and married graduate
students. Two-thirds of all apartments occupy building corners
and so enjoy double exposure; an arresting Picasso sculpture lends
drama to the development's central space. Senior associate in
charge: James Ingo Freed. Engineers: Farkas & Barron (structural); Caretsky Associates (mechanical). General contractor:
Tishman Construction Corporation. HONORS: AIA Honor Award,
1967; Bard Award, 1967. SEE: Architectural Forum (vol. 125)
December 1966, 21-29.

---

I. M. PEI; COSSUTA & PONTE

---

222. Christian Science Church Center; Boston, MA; 1971/1973. Incorporated into an already existing complex on a 15-acre site are a

30.  University Plaza.  I. M. Pei.
     Photo:  © Ashod Kassabian 1981

28-story Church Administration tower, a 525-foot long, five-story high Colonnade Building and a trim three-story Sunday School. Set among them are formal gardens and a 670-foot long reflecting pool. Associate in charge: Joseph V. Morog. Engineers: Weiskopf & Pickworth (structural); Syska & Hennessy (mechanical/electrical). Landscape architects: Sasaki, Dawson, DeMay Associates. General contractor: Aberthaw Construction Co. HONORS: AIA Bicentennial List, 2 nominations. SEE: Architectural Forum (vol. 139) September 1973, 24-39.

## I. M. PEI; KING & KING

223. School of Journalism Building, Syracuse University; Syracuse, NY; 1964. This concrete building with a neoclassic air was designed to be the first of three in the Samuel I. Newhouse Communications Center. As the key structure in a projected quadrangle, it was set on a raised plaza; facilities that required no natural light and might be shared by the other two buildings were located centrally under the plaza. Architect in charge for I. M. Pei & Associates: Kellogg Wong. Associated project architect for King & King: Russell King. Engineers: Eckerlin & Klepper (structural); Robson & Woese (mechanical). General contractor: J. D. Taylor Construction Co. HONORS: AIA First Honor Award, 1965. SEE: Progressive Architecture (vol. 46) February 1965, 168-173. AIA Journal (vol. 44) July 1965, 23-46.

## PEREIRA & LUCKMAN

224. Beckman, Helipot Corporation plant; Newport Beach, CA; 1957/1958. An industrial plant that resembles a resort hotel, geared to blend into a seaside town and attract high caliber personnel. Designed for the manufacture of precision electronic components, it supplies high levels of light and close control of temperature, humidity and dust. Landscape architect: Fred Lang. Contractor: M. J. Brock & Sons. HONORS: AIA Merit Award, 1958. SEE: Arts and Architecture (vol. 75) May 1958, 10-11. Architectural Record (vol. 125) January 1959, 147-170.

225. C. B. S. Television City; Los Angeles, CA; 1952. A complex of studios and related facilities for producing programs for TV. Studios are enormous: 130 x 110 x 42 feet high; hung from their ceilings are intricate systems of movable lights, cameras and air conditioning vents. General contractor: William Simpson Construction

Company. HONORS: AIA Merit Award, 1954. SEE: Architectural Forum (vol. 96) May 1952, 101-110. Architectural Forum (vol. 98) March 1953, 146-149.

PERKINS & WILL

226. Keokuk Senior High School and Community College; Keokuk, IA. Spread out on a generous site in rolling grasslands, this school incorporates energy efficient features such as sunshades and through ventilation. Along one long side of its four-story classroom building, glass-walled corridors highlighted by red sun fins and yellow window frames give students inside beautiful views while presenting a lively and colorful facade. Landscape architect: David Gill. General contractor: Lovejoy Construction Co. HONORS: AIA Merit Award, 1954. SEE: Architectural Forum (vol. 101) October 1954, 113-119.

WILLIAM WESLEY PETERS see FRANK LLOYD WRIGHT; WILLIAM WESLEY PETERS and TALIESIN ASSOCIATED ARCHITECTS

PETERSON & BRICKBAUER

227. Maryland Blue Cross Inc.; Towson, MD; 1972. At this jauntily imaginative headquarters in a suburban setting, offices are housed in a mirrored cube 134 feet square by 134 feet tall while mechanical services occupy a flame red brick-faced 42-foot cube alongside. Associate architects: Brown, Guenther, Battaglia, Galvin. Engineers: Sadler Associates (structural); Piccirillo & Brown (mechanical/electrical). General contractor: The Cogswell Construction Co. SEE: Architecture Plus (vol. 1) April 1973, 16-21.

PIERCE & PIERCE see GOLEMAN & ROLFE; PIERCE & PIERCE

## JAMES STEWART POLSHEK

228. New York State Bar Center; Albany, NY; 1971. Three historic row-houses were incorporated into the tasteful design of this bar association headquarters which contains office space and a Great Hall used for large receptions and as a library/lounge. New structures are placed deferentially behind the old; large spaces, skylighted, are located underneath a modified courtyard. Associate in charge: Howard M. Kaplan. Landscape architects: Johnson and Dee. Engineers: Aaron Garfinkel Associates (structural); Benjamin & Zicherman (mechanical/electrical). General contractor: McManus, Longe, Brockwehl, Inc. HONORS: PA Design Award, 1969; AIA Honor Award, 1972. SEE: Architectural Record (vol. 150) December 1971, 94-99.

## POMERANCE & BREINES

229. Amphitheater and Plaza, Jacob Riis Houses; New York, NY; 1966. Three acres of inviting--and virtually indestructible--facilities for outdoor recreation in the heart of a low income housing development. Included in this mostly hard-paved space are a sculptural fountain, an amphitheater, a sequence of open air "rooms" and lots of things to climb on. Landscape architect: M. Paul Friedberg & Assoc. Engineers: Ames & Selnick (structural); I. M. Robbins & Assoc. (mechanical). General contractor: W. J. Barney. HONORS: AIA Honor Award, 1967; Bard Award, 1967. SEE: Architectural Forum (vol. 125) July-August 1966, 68-[73].

## JOHN PORTMAN
See also EDWARDS & PORTMAN.

230. Hyatt Regency San Francisco, Embarcadero Center; San Francisco, CA; 1972. A breathtakingly huge and lovingly detailed prism-shaped interior space 17 stories high and 300 feet long is the focus of this 840-room hotel located in a gala downtown office/shopping/restaurant complex. Many of its rooms, poised on one sharply sloping facade, look out on a fountain designed by Lawrence Halprin. Mechanical engineers: Britt Alderman, Jr. & Assoc. General contractors: Jones-Allen-Dillingham, a joint venture of J. A. Jones Construction Co., J. B. Allen Co. and

Dillingham Corp.  HONORS:  AIA Bicentennial List, 2 nominations.
SEE:  Architectural Forum (vol. 140) November 1973, [46]-55.  Y.
Futagawa, ed., John Portman ... Hyatt Regency San Francisco.
Text by Paul Goldberger.  (Global Architecture, no. 28.)  Tokyo:
A. D. A.  Edita, 1974.

231.  Los Angeles Bonaventure Hotel; Los Angeles, CA; 1976.  An eye
catcher for Tinseltown:  a hotel in the shape of five glittering,
mirrored cylinders, 30 to 37 stories high.  It contains almost
1500 rooms and suites plus a multitude of shops and restaurants
including a restaurant and revolving bar at the top of its central
cylinder.  Consultants:  Everett Conklin-West (landscape architects); John Blum & Assoc. (structural engineers); Britt Alderman
Engineers (mechanical engineers).  General contractors:  C. L.
Peck in joint venture with Henry C. Beck Co.  SEE:  Progressive
Architecture (vol. 59) February 1978, 52-56.  Y. Futagawa, ed.,
John Portman & Associates ... Los Angeles Bonaventure Hotel ...
Renaissance Center.  Text by Paul Goldberger.  (Global Architec-
ture, no. 57.)  Tokyo:  A. D. A.  Edita, 1981.

232.  Renaissance Center; Detroit, MI; 1977.  A 32-acre riverfront complex, nicknamed RenCen, that includes a shopping mall and convention facilities.  At its center, the Detroit Plaza Hotel rises
73 stories, a shiny cylinder sheathed in reflective glass.  Sym-
metrically arranged around it are four octagonal office towers.
Consultants:  John Grissim & Assoc. (landscape architects); Britt
Alderman Associates (mechanical).  General contractor:  Tishman
Construction Co.  SEE:  AIA Journal (vol. 68) September 1977,
28-31.  Progressive Architecture (vol. 59) February 1978, 57-61.
Y. Futagawa, ed., John Portman & Associates:  ... Los Angeles
Bonaventure Hotel ... Renaissance Center.  Text by Paul Gold-
berger.  (Global Architecture, no. 57.)  Tokyo:  A. D. A.  Edita,
1981.

QUINN & ODA

233.  Church of Our Divine Savior; Chico, CA; 1970.  An inviting small
church, built on a tiny budget, to serve a neighborhood of trailer
parks and modest homes.  The sanctuary can seat as many as 370
or can be divided into two spaces; the altar is movable.  HONORS:
AIA Honor Award, 1971; Bartlett Award, 1971.  SEE:  AIA Journal (vol. 55) June 1971, 45-55.  Architectural Record (vol. 154)
July 1973, 117-132.

RALPH RAPSON

234. Cedar Square West; Minneapolis, MN; 1974. A 1299-unit residential complex of 11 buildings ranging from 4 to 40 stories and designed to serve as the nucleus for a "new town in town" to be known as Cedar-Riverside. Curiously, although this development quickly found satisfied tenants, its expansion was fiercely opposed by community groups. Engineers: Crosier, Greenberg & Partners (structural); Egan & Sons (mechanical). Landscape architect: Sasaki, Walker Associates. General contractor: Borson Construction Co. HONORS: AIA Honor Award, 1975; Bartlett Award, 1975; AIA Bicentennial List, 1 nomination. SEE: Architectural Record (vol. 154) December 1973, 102-103. AIA Journal (vol. 62) December 1974, 33-35. AIA Journal (vol. 63) May 1975, 28.

235. Tyrone Guthrie Theater; Minneapolis, MN; 1963. This innovative theater has an asymmetrical open stage which can accommodate backdrops at the rear yet is surrounded by seating on three sides. None of its 1437 seats, also asymmetrically arranged, is more than 15 rows from the stage. Project coordinator: Gene Stuart Peterson. Engineers: Meyer & Borgman (structural); Oftedal, Locke & Broadston (mechanical). Acoustical consultant: Robert F. Lambert. HONORS: PA Design Citation, 1961. SEE: Progressive Architecture (vol. 44) December 1963, [98]-[105] and cover.

JOHN LYON REID

236. Hillsdale High School; San Mateo, CA; 1955. An unusual school built around a giant courtyard that encompasses a small, simple stadium with two pools. Classrooms are located in two factory-like blocks of flexible loft space; many have no windows but are illuminated by skylights. Partner in charge: Burton Rockwell. Structural engineers: Alexander G. Tarics. Landscape architects: Eckbo, Royston & Williams. General contractors: Rothschild, Raffin & Weirick and Northern Constructors. HONORS: AIA Honor Award, 1956. SEE: Architectural Forum (vol. 104) January 1956, 134-139. Architectural Forum (vol. 105) August 1956, 134-139.

REID, ROCKWELL, BANWELL & TARICS

237. Health Sciences Instruction and Research Towers, Unit 1, San

Francisco Medical Center, University of California; San Francisco, CA; 1966/1967. Twin 16-story towers built on a very constricted site provide column-free laboratory space 90 feet square, unhampered by a complex system of ducts positioned externally. Glass-walled perimeter corridors help to insulate the labs while making the most of attractive views. Mechanical/electrical engineers: DeLeuw, Cather & Co. General contractor: Dinwiddie Construction Co. HONORS: PA Design Citation, 1961; AISC Architectural Award of Excellence, 1967; AIA Honor Award, 1968. SEE: Architectural Record (vol. 143) June 1968, 129-134.

## VILJO REVELL; JOHN B. PARKIN ASSOCIATES

238. Toronto City Hall; Toronto, Canada; 1965. Built from a design that won over more than 500 others in an international competition, this remarkable City Hall looks like an eye from above: its two crescent office towers enfold a low, circular council chamber. Its spacious forecourt is marked by a sweeping ramp, an elevated walkway and a pool designed to be used for skating in winter. Engineers: Severud-Elstad-Kreuger Associates (structural); Jaros, Baum & Bolles (mechanical). Landscape architects: Sasaki Strong & Assoc. Acoustic consultant: Prof. V. L. Henderson. General contractors: Anglin-Norcross (Ontario) Limited. SEE: Architectural Forum (vol. 123) November 1965, 15-[23]. Architectural Record (vol. 138) November 1965, 165-172.

## REYNOLDS, SMITH & HILLS

239. Tampa International Airport; Tampa, FL; 1971. This airport features an elevated transit system which shuttles travelers between a central "Landside" terminal building and "Airside" emplaning facilities arranged in a semicircle around it. Officer in charge: Ivan H. Smith. General engineering consultant: J. E. Greiner Co. General contractors: McDevitt & Street Co.; J. A. Jones Construction Co.; C. A. Fielland, Inc. SEE: Architectural Forum (vol. 135) October 1971, [34]-[37].

## RHONE & IREDALE

240. Sedgewick Library, University of British Columbia; Vancouver, B.C.,

Canada; 1972. To locate this terraced, largely underground library centrally on campus while preserving a distinctive row of eight oak trees, a drum 30 feet in diameter was constructed around the roots of each tree and extended from mall level down through the building's lower floors. Interior study spaces were boldly varied and include "carpeted nooks and crannies suitable for very informal postures" as well as more formal areas enlivened by vivid graphics. Partner in charge: Randle Iredale. Consultants: Canadian Environmental Science (structural/landscaping); D. W. Thomson & Co. (mechanical/electrical). General contractor: Cana Construction. HONORS: Canadian Architect Yearbook Award, 1970. SEE: Canadian Architect (vol. 18) April 1973, 40-45. A + U: Architecture and Urbanism (no. 50) February 1975, 55-62. Process: Architecture (no. 5) 1978, 94-101.

RICHARDSON ASSOCIATES

241. Sea-Tac International Airport Expansion; near Seattle, WA; 1974. For heightened convenience, facilites at this airport are interconnected by an automated transit system for passengers and an integrated baggage handling system. A 4300-car garage is located within the chevron shape of the main terminal. Project architect: Allen D. Moses. Engineer consultants: Victor O. Gray & Co., Andersen, Bjornstad & Kane (structural); Miskimen/Associates (mechanical). Landscape consultants: Sasaki, Walker & Associates. General contractor, passenger terminal: Morrison-Knudsen Company. SEE: Architectural Record (vol. 154) November 1973, 135-152.

KEVIN ROCHE JOHN DINKELOO
Winner of the AIA's Architectural Firm Award for 1974.

242. College Life Insurance Company of America; Indianapolis, IN; 1971, first phase. In this complex, three monolithic, 11-story office buildings, almost pyramidal in shape, are linked together by bridges and overlook a man-made lake. Windowless concrete walls predominate in their design but one sloping side of each building is sheathed in reflective glass. Engineers: Severud Associates (structural); Hubbard, Lawless & Osborne (mechanical/electrical). General contractor: Mid Republic Construction, Inc. SEE: Architectural Forum (vol. 140) March 1974, 26-31. Y. Futagawa, ed., Kevin Roche John Dinkeloo ... College Life Insurance Company Headquarters.... Text by William Marlin. (Global Architecture, no. 29.) Tokyo: A.D.A. Edita, 1974.

243.   Deere West, John Deere and Company Administrative Center; Moline, IL; 1978.   A long steel-framed, glassed-in bridge connects this three-level, weathering steel addition to a seven-level corporate headquarters of similar construction designed by Eero Saarinen (q. v. ) and completed in 1964.   Within Deere West there's a quarter-acre, glass-roofed, multi-level garden used in part for "outdoor" dining; an inviting cafeteria and other attractive eating areas are located nearby.   Mechanical engineers:  AZCO Downey, Inc.  Consultants:  Tropical Plant Rental, Inc. (garden landscaping); Lankenau-Damgaard & Assoc. (exterior landscaping).   General contractor:  Turner Construction Co.   SEE:  Architectural Record (vol. 165) February 1979, 85-92.   AIA Journal (vol. 68) Mid-May 1979, 138-145.

244.   Ford Foundation Building; New York, NY; 1967 (Illus. 31).   Behind this prizewinner's serene granite and glass facade lies an elegantly wrought and richly fitted 12-story office building with a one-third acre garden within it, enclosed by walls of glass.   Offices are grouped around this many-leveled courtyard to enhance the staff's sense of community.   Associates:  Eugene Festa, Philip Kinsella.   Engineers:  Severud Associates (structural); Cosentini Associates (mechanical).   Landscape architect:  Dan Kiley.   General contractor:  Turner Construction Co.   HONORS:  Bard Award, 1968; AIA Bicentennial List, 11 nominations.   SEE:  Architectural Record (vol. 143) February 1968, 105-[112] and cover.   Y. Futagawa, ed., Kevin Roche John Dinkeloo and Associates:  The Ford Foundation Building ... The Oakland Museum....  Text by William Marlin.  (Global Architecture, no. 4. )  Tokyo:  A. D. A. Edita, 1974.   Y. Futagawa, ed., Kevin Roche John Dinkeloo:  The Ford Foundation Headquarters....  Text by Nobuo Hozumi.  (Global Architecture Detail, no. 4. )  Tokyo:  A. D. A. Edita, 1977.

245.   Knights of Columbus Headquarters; New Haven, CT; 1970.   A 23-story office building primarily faced with glass shaded by massive overhangs of weathering steel, it has at its four corners tile-sheathed, circular concrete columns which contain lavatories and fire stairs and which, in conjunction with the building's elevator core, support its structural girders.   Steel overhangs are omitted from its more gently handled bottom three stories.   Project associates:  David Powrie, Bruce Detmers.   Engineers:  Pfisterer, Tor & Associates (structural); Cosentini Associates (mechanical).   General contractor:  Koppers Company, Inc.   HONORS:  AISC Architectural Award of Excellence, 1970.   SEE:  Architectural Record (vol. 148) August 1970, 109-116.   Progressive Architecture (vol. 51) September 1970, 84-[91].

246.   Oakland Museum; Oakland, CA; 1969.   This wide ranging complex-- built on a four-block site and comprising art, cultural history and natural science galleries on three separate levels--is elaborately terraced and ingratiatingly landscaped.   Much of its exhibition space is underground while plantings on its terraces and greenery

31. Ford Foundation Building.  Roche, Dinkeloo.
Photo: © 1967 Ezra Stoller (Esto); courtesy of the Ford Foundation

on top endow it with many of the qualities of a botanical garden. Associate on job: Philip Kinsella. Engineers: Severud Associates (structural); Alexander Boome (mechanical/electrical). Landscape architect: Dan Kiley. Contractor: B & R Construction Co. HONORS: AIA Bicentennial List, 1 nomination. SEE: Architectural Record (vol. 147) April 1970, 115-122. Y. Futagawa, ed., Kevin Roche John Dinkeloo and Associates: The Ford Foundation Building ... The Oakland Museum.... Text by William Marlin. (Global Architecture, no. 4.) Tokyo: A. D. A. Edita, 1974.

247. Veterans Memorial Coliseum; New Haven, CT; 1972. This "big, brawny building," which can seat as many as 11,500 spectators, is situated in the heart of a downtown redevelopment area, adjacent to the Knights of Columbus Headquarters (see entry no. 245) designed by the same architectural firm. Spanning its arena is a four-level parking garage reached by two giant spiral ramps. Engineers: Le Messurier Associates (structural); Hubbard, Lawless & Osborne (mechanical/electrical). Acoustical consultants: Bolt, Beranek & Newman. General contractor: Gilbane Building Co. SEE: Architectural Review (vol. 153) April 1973, [216]-232. Architectural Forum (vol. 140) March 1974, 36-41.

SIMON RODILLA, also known as SAM RODIA

248. Watts Towers; Los Angeles, CA; 1954. One man's artistic fantasy given substance: fanciful spires pieced together over a period of 33 years from steel reinforcing rods and wire mesh colorfully decorated with seashells and fragments of broken dishes and bottles. HONORS: AIA Bicentennial List, 1 nomination. SEE: Architectural Review (vol. 68) July 1951, 23-25. Arts and Architecture (vol. 76) September 1959, 27-28. Architectural Forum (vol. 123) September 1965, 19. Process: Architecture (no. 3) December 1977, 224-225.

EMERY ROTH AND SONS
See also entry no. 377.

249. Pan Am Building; New York, NY; 1963. A controversial, prism-shaped, giant office building--a 49-story tower on a 10-story base--which was erected just north of the stately old Grand Central Terminal and so visually obstructed Park Avenue. It was designed to accommodate 17,000 occupants and 250,000 visitors daily. Design consultants: Walter Gropius, Pietro Belluschi. Engineers: James

Ruderman (structural); Jaros, Baum & Bolles (mechanical/electrical). General contractor: Diesel Construction Co. SEE: Progressive Architecture (vol. 44) April 1963, 59-62. Architectural Record (vol. 133) May 1963, [151]-158.

---

## BERNARD ROTHZEID
   Subsequent firm name: ROTHZEID KAISERMAN & THOMSON

---

250. Turtle Bay Towers; New York, NY; 1977 (Illus. 32). Here's an imaginative renovation in which a 24-story factory loft building, badly damaged by a gas explosion, has been transformed into luxury housing. Greenhouse extensions tucked into the building's setbacks give attractive added space to its roomy, high-ceilinged apartments. Partner in charge: Peter Thomson; project designers: Bernard Rothzeid, Carmi Bee. Engineers: Harwood & Gould (structural); George Langer (mechanical/electrical). General contractor: Rockrose Construction Corporation. HONORS: AIA Honor Award for Extended Use, 1978; Bard Award, 1979. SEE: Architectural Record (vol. 162) September 1977, [111]-[126]. AIA Journal (vol. 67) Mid-May 1978, 134-[135].

---

## PAUL RUDOLPH

---

251. Boston Government Service Center; Boston, MA. 1971. A monumental megastructure shaped, in plan, like a hollow wedge and built around an elegantly contoured plaza. It comprises the Division of Employment Security Building (Shepley, Bulfinch, Richardson & Abbott, architects); Mental Health Building (Desmond & Lord, architects) and the Health, Welfare and Education Building (M. A. Dyer and Pedersen & Tilney, architects). Coordinating architect, architectural designer for the Mental Health and Health, Welfare and Education Buildings, and architect for the garage and plaza: Paul Rudolph. Engineers: Souza & True (structural); Greenleaf Associates (mechanical/electrical). SEE: Architectural Record (vol. 139) June 1966, 140-141. L'Architecture d'Aujourd'hui (no. 157) August 1971, 88-91. Y. Futagawa, ed., Paul Rudolph: Interdenominational Chapel, Tuskegee ... Boston Government Service Center.... Text by Carl Black, Jr. (Global Architecture, no. 20.) Tokyo: A.D.A. Edita, 1973.

252. Endo Laboratories Building; Garden City, Long Island, NY; 1964. A pharmaceutical manufacturing plant designed to keep its skilled workers happy while providing them with interior spaces tailored

32. Turtle Bay Towers.   Bernard Rothzeid.
Photo:  Norman McGrath

for particular job functions. Its cast-in-place concrete facade, approached by a long, almost ceremonial staircase, is marked by rows of fortress-like turrets. For meals and breaks there's an appealing roof garden topped off by a spacious glass-enclosed pavilion. Job captain: Bryant L. Conant. Structural engineer: Henry A. Pfisterer. Mechanical engineer and general contractor: Walter Kidde Constructors, Inc. Landscape architects: Robert Zion-Harold Breen. SEE: Progressive Architecture (vol. 45) November 1964, 168-173. The Architecture of Paul Rudolph. Introduction by Sibyl Moholy-Nagy ... with comments by Paul Rudolph. New York: Praeger, 1970.

253. Married Student Housing, Yale University; New Haven, CT; 1961. Five low-rise apartment units faced in tweedy-textured brick are arranged irregularly around a flight of steps that almost bisects their steep site. This unusual small housing development is said to have been inspired by Mediterranean hillside villages. Engineers: Henry Pfisterer (structural); Van Zelm, Heywood & Shadford (mechanical/electrical). General contractor: G. B. H. Macomber Co. SEE: Architectural Record (vol. 129) March 1961, 139-154. Architectural Forum (vol. 116) March 1962, [98]-[101].

254. Mary Cooper Jewett Arts Center, Wellesley College; Wellesley, MA; 1959. A contemporary building whose lines, color and scale fit in gracefully on a red brick and limestone Collegiate Gothic campus. Its three main elements are a two-story music/drama unit which includes an auditorium, a taller and narrower visual arts unit set at right angles to it, and an exhibition gallery that seams together the art and music units while it serves as a foyer for the auditorium. Associate architects: Anderson, Beckwith & Haible. Engineers: Goldberg, Le Messurier & Associates (structural); Stressenger, Adams, Maguire & Reidy (mechanical/electrical). Acoustical consultants: Bolt, Beranek & Newman. General contractor: George A. Fuller Co. SEE: Architectural Record (vol. 126) July 1959, 175-186.

255. Orange County Government Center; Goshen, NY; 1970. Inside and out this low, complex building displays geometric yet determinedly irregular lines. Constructed of exposed concrete and split-rib concrete block, it houses courtrooms of varying sizes--seating from 24 to 125 spectators--plus associated offices and other facilities. Project architects: William Bedford, James Brown. Engineers: Lev Zetlin Associates (structural); Caretsky & Assoc. (mechanical/electrical). General contractor: Corbeau-Newman Construction Corporation. SEE: Architectural Record (vol. 150) August 1971, 83-92.

256. Sarasota Senior High School; Sarasota, FL; 1959/1960. Well designed for a tropical climate, this school was sited on a hill, oriented north-south, and cleverly ventilated and provided with sunshades to make the most of prevailing breezes while shielding students from excessive glare and heat. Engineers: Sidney L.

Barker (structural); Charles T. Healy (mechanical). Contractor: Coe Construction Co. HONORS: AIA Merit Award, 1962. SEE: Architectural Record (vol. 125) March 1959, 189-194. Architectural Record (vol. 127) May 1960, 193-216.

257. School of Art and Architecture, Yale University; New Haven, CT; 1963. This intricate, complex building's plan has been likened by its architect to that of a pinwheel. Constructed of rough-surfaced concrete inside and out, it boasts a wide variety of exciting interior spaces, some of them adorned by casts of works of art such as classic statues and Louis Sullivan friezes. Engineers: Henry A. Pfisterer (structural); vanZelm, Heywood & Shadford (mechanical). General contractor: George B. H. Macomber Co. HONORS: AIA First Honor Award, 1964; AIA 1976 Bicentennial List, 4 nominations. SEE: Progressive Architecture (vol. 45) February 1964, [106]-[127]. Architectural Review (vol. 135) May 1964, [324]-[332].

258. Temple Street Parking Garage; New Haven, CT; 1962/1963. Two blocks long, five levels high, spare yet with a look of formidable authority, here is a car park with a difference. Modeled out of cast-in-place concrete, its levels--rounded shelves without walls-- rise on a series of gracefully molded pillars. Engineers: Henry Pfisterer (structural); Jerome Mueller (mechanical). General contractor: Fusco-Amatruda Co. HONORS: AIA Merit Award, 1964. SEE: Architectural Forum (vol. 118) February 1963, 104-[109]. Architectural Record (vol. 133) February 1963, 145-[150].

---

PAUL RUDOLPH; DESMOND & LORD

---

259. Southeastern Massachusetts University (formerly Southeastern Massachusetts Technological Institute); North Dartmouth, MA; master plan and first stage, 1966. A campus whose configuration resembles Venice's Piazza San Marco and includes a central tower like the Piazza's Campanile. Buildings are constructed of concrete and are tidily ornamented inside and out with ribbed concrete block; they spiral around the tower down the hillside and look out through trees to a nearby lake. Job captain: Grattan Gill. Structural engineers: Congdon, Gurney & Towle. Structural consultant: Sepp Firnkas. General contractor: Franchi Construction Co. SEE: Architectural Record (vol. 140) October 1966, [145]-160. Architectural Record (vol. 157) January 1975, 123-140.

## PAUL RUDOLPH; FRY & WELCH

260. Chapel, Tuskegee Institute; Tuskegee, AL; 1969. Central to the campus of an historic Negro college, this church was erected to replace one which had burned down a dozen years before. Its sharply angled, almost windowless exterior conceals a high lofting, asymmetrical sanctuary which has been called "one of the most dramatic and powerful spaces to be built in this century." Architects and planners: Fry & Welch. Associate architect (design phase): Paul Rudolph. Engineers: Donald J. Neubauer (structural); A. Dee Counts (mechanical). Acoustical consultants: Bolt, Beranek & Newman. Contractors: George B. H. Macomber Co.; F. N. Thompson, Inc. SEE: Architectural Record (vol. 146) November 1969, 117-126. Y. Futagawa, ed., Paul Rudolph: Interdenominational Chapel, Tuskegee ... Boston Government Service Center.... Text by Carl Black, Jr. (Global Architecture, no. 20.) Tokyo: A.D.A. Edita, 1973.

## GEORGE VERNON RUSSELL

261. Republic Supply Company Offices and Plant; San Leandro, CA; 1952. A multi-purpose industrial building constructed on a modest budget yet attractive to employees and customers. Graciously landscaped, it features a large patio--bounded by two wings of offices--which can be used as a lounge, for meetings and for outdoor dining. Landscape architect: Lawrence Halprin. Contractor: Swinerton & Walberg Co. HONORS: AIA Merit Award, 1953. SEE: Architectural Forum (vol. 99) August 1953, 107-109.

## EERO SAARINEN
Winner, AIA Gold Medal, 1962.

262. Bell Telephone Laboratories Research Center; Holmdel, NJ; 1966. Sited on 456 rural acres, this is an immense office/laboratory facility: 700 feet long, 350 feet wide and six stories high with a 700 by 100 foot central covered garden. Though it was one of the first buildings to be completely sheathed in reflective glass, none of its labs or offices have windows; continuous corridors around its perimeter lessen problems of climate control. Landscape architects: Sasaki-Dawson-DeMay Associates. Engineers: Severud

Associates (structural); Jaros, Baum & Bolles (mechanical/electrical). SEE: Architectural Forum (vol. 117) October 1962, 88-[97]. Architectural Forum (vol. 126) April 1967, 33-[41]. Y. Futagawa, ed., Eero Saarinen: Bell Telephone Corporation Research Laboratories ... Deere & Company Headquarters.... Text by Cesar Pelli and Diana Pelli. (Global Architecture, no. 6.) Tokyo: A.D.A. Edita, 1971.

263. CBS Building; New York, NY; 1965 (Illus. 33). A 38-story, rectangular office tower of determined simplicity set off from its neighbors by a sunken plaza. On all four of its sides, closely spaced triangular pillars faced with dark gray granite run without interruption from ground level to roof. Engineers: Paul Weidlinger (structural); Cosentini Associates (mechanical). General contractor: George A. Fuller Co. HONORS: AIA Honor Award, 1966; AIA Bicentennial List, 2 nominations. SEE: Progressive Architecture (vol. 46) July 1965, [187]-192. Architectural Forum (vol. 124) April 1966, [28]-[37].

264. Concordia Senior College; Fort Wayne, IN; 1958. In designing this wholly new campus for a college with 450 Lutheran preministerial students, Saarinen's goal was to create a kind of tranquil, self-sufficient village. All its buildings have pitched, dark gray tile roofs and are constructed of reinforced concrete plus nonbearing whitewashed brick; the simple chapel is particularly noteworthy. Engineers: Severud-Elstad-Krueger (structural); Samuel R. Lewis & Assoc. (mechanical). Landscape architect: Dan Kiley. General contractors: Wermuth, Inc.; Hagerman Construction Corp.; Grewe Contractors, Inc. HONORS: PA Design Award, 1956; AIA Honor Award, 1959. SEE: Progressive Architecture (vol. 39) December 1958, 88-101.

265. David S. Ingalls Hockey Rink, Yale University; New Haven, CT; 1958. This remarkable building--whose shape has been compared to that of a Viking warship or a giant dinosaur--is a study in dramatic curves and adventurous engineering. It seats 2900 for hockey matches, as many as 5000 for lectures and commencement exercises, and has excellent acoustics. Associate architect: Douglas W. Orr. Engineers: Severud-Elstad-Krueger Associates (structural); Jaros, Baum & Bolles (mechanical/electrical). General contractor: George B. H. Macomber Co. HONORS: AIA Bicentennial List, 1 nomination. SEE: Architectural Record (vol. 124) October 1958, 151-158. Architectural Forum (vol. 109) December 1958, 106-111.

266. Deere & Company Administrative Center; Moline, IL; 1964. This headquarters for a farm equipment manufacturer pioneered in the use of weathering steel--high-tensile steel which, if left unpainted, forms its own cinnamon brown protective coating. Set on a wooded site with two man-made lakes, its three original facilities were an auditorium, an office building and a display building, the latter two

33. CBS Building.
    Eero Saarinen.
    Photo: courtesy
    of CBS Inc.

connected by a bridge across a ravine. Their strong yet artfully detailed lines bear a curious resemblance to Japanese temple architecture. See also Deere West (entry no. 243), designed by Kevin Roche John Dinkeloo, successor firm to Eero Saarinen & Assoc. Engineers: Ammann & Whitney (structural); Burns & McDonnell Engineering Co. (mechanical/electrical). Landscape architects: Sasaki, Walker & Assoc. General contractor: Huber, Hunt & Nichols. HONORS: AIA Honor Award, 1965; AIA Bicentennial List, 3 nominations. SEE: Architectural Forum (vol. 121) July 1964, [76]-[85]. Architectural Record (vol. 136) July 1964, 135-142. Y. Futagawa, ed., Eero Saarinen: Bell Telephone Corporation Research Laboratories ... Deere & Company Headquarters .... Text by Cesar Pelli and Diana Pelli. (Global Architecture, no. 6.) Tokyo: A.D.A. Edita, 1971.

267. Dulles International Airport Terminal Building; Chantilly, VA; 1962. Set on a huge (10,000 acres) flat site, this is a highly distinctive building with colonnades of tipped and tapered columns on its two long facades, a gracefully curving roof hung between them, and a pagoda-like control tower nearby. Mobile lounges are used to carry passengers from the terminal to their planes. Engineers: Ammann & Whitney (structural); Burns & McDonnell Engineering Co. (mechanical/electrical). Landscape architect: Dan Kiley. Contractors: Humphreys & Harding; Corbetta Construction Co. HONORS: AIA Honor Award, 1966; AIA Bicentennial List, 17 nominations. SEE: Architectural Record (vol. 134) July 1963, 101-110. Progressive Architecture (vol. 44) August 1963, [86]-101. Y. Futagawa, ed., Eero Saarinen: TWA Terminal Building ... Dulles International Airport.... Text by Nobuo Hozumi. (Global Architecture, no. 26.) Tokyo: A.D.A. Edita, 1973.

268. Gateway Arch; St. Louis, MO; 1965/1968. Part of the Jefferson National Expansion Memorial, this remarkable, tapered arch symbolizes the role of St. Louis as gateway to the West. It is 630 feet high, measures 630 feet across at its base, and is constructed of a steel double wall filled with concrete at its lower levels and stiffened with steel further up where it is narrower. Its exterior is clad in polished stainless steel. Landscape architect: Dan Kiley. HONORS: AISC Architectural Award of Excellence, 1967; AIA Bicentennial List, 9 nominations. SEE: Architectural Forum (vol. 128) June 1968, 32-37. George McCue, The Building Art in St. Louis: Two Centuries. St. Louis Chapter, American Institute of Architects, 1964. Joel Meyerowitz, St. Louis and the Arch. Boston: N.Y. Graphic Society, 1980.

269. Kresge Auditorium, Massachusetts Institute of Technology; Cambridge, MA; 1955. This "festival hall on the banks of the Charles River" contains a little theater, a concert hall and rehearsal rooms. It is noted for its graceful white dome: one-eighth of a sphere anchored on hidden abutments at three points. On the three faces between, glass walls arch upward to meet its thin concrete shell.

Associate architects: Anderson & Beckwith. Engineers: Ammann & Whitney (structural); Hyde & Bobbio (mechanical/electrical); Bolt, Beranek & Newman (acoustical). General contractor: George A. Fuller Co. SEE: Architectural Forum (vol. 103) July 1955, 128-129. Architectural Record (vol. 118) July 1955 (131-137).

270. Kresge Chapel, Massachusetts Institute of Technology; Cambridge, MA; 1955. This interdenominational chapel built on a small hemmed-in site masterfully achieves an atmosphere conducive to meditation. Reached by a glassed-in walkway that crosses a tiny moat, on the outside it's a windowless, brick-faced cylinder; inside, its brick walls undulate gently and natural light comes in indirectly from the sides and above. Associate architects: Anderson & Beckwith. Engineers: Ammann & Whitney (structural); Hyde & Bobbio (mechanical/electrical); Bolt, Beranek & Newman (acoustical). General contractor: George A. Fuller Co. HONORS: AIA Bicentennial List, 1 nomination. SEE: Architectural Forum (vol. 104) January 1956, 116-121. Architectural Record (vol. 119) January 1956, 154-157.

271. Milwaukee County War Memorial; Milwaukee, WI; 1957. Shaped like a hollow cross, this unusual community center contains meeting rooms, an auditorium and an art gallery; the memorial courtyard at its center overlooks Lake Michigan through the building's supporting pylons. When first built, its engineering was considered daring since its two upper floors cantilever out over 29 feet. Associated architects: Maynard W. Meyer & Assoc. Engineers: Ammann & Whitney (structural); Samuel R. Lewis & Assoc. (mechanical). General contractor: James McHugh Construction Co. HONORS: PA Award Citation, 1955. SEE: Architectural Forum (vol. 107) December 1957, 90-[95], 144.

272. Samuel F. B. Morse and Ezra Stiles Colleges, Yale University; New Haven, CT; 1962. Because Yale students preferred Gothic rooms to Georgian on campus, the architect set out to design these residence halls--which contain dining halls, lounges and small libraries as well as bedrooms--as "citadels of earthy monolithic masonry." Medium-rise buildings set in rambling fashion around courtyards, their concrete construction is relieved by decorative sculpture and by interior detailing in stone and oak. Engineers: Henry A. Pfisterer (structural); Van Zelm, Heywood & Shadford (mechanical). Landscape architect: Dan Kiley. General contractor: E & F Construction Co. HONORS: AIA Honor Award, 1963. SEE: Architectural Forum (vol. 117) December 1962, 105-111. Architectural Record (vol. 132) December 1962, 93-100.

273. TWA Terminal, Kennedy (formerly Idlewild) International Airport; New York, NY; 1962 (Illus. 34). Surely one of the world's most dramatic airline terminals. Few straight lines here: approached head on, its curving contours uncannily suggest a bird in flight. Inside, the main lobby's soaring, swooping walls, its carefully modeled staircases, seating areas and many other features are a

34.   TWA Terminal, Kennedy International Airport.   Eero Saarinen.
Photo:   courtesy of TWA Skyliner

blend of graceful sculptural forms selected "to suggest the excite-
ment of the trip." Engineers: Ammann & Whitney (structural);
Jaros, Baum & Bolles (mechanical).  Contractor: Grove, Shepherd,
Wilson & Kruger.  HONORS: AIA Merit Award, 1963; AIA Bicen-
tennial List, 3 nominations.  SEE: Architectural Record (vol. 130)
September 1961, 162-164.  Architectural Forum (vol. 117) July
1962, 72-75.  Progressive Architecture (vol. 43) October 1962,
158-165.  Y. Futagawa, ed., Eero Saarinen: TWA Terminal
Building Kennedy Airport ... Dulles International Airport....
Text by Nobuo Hozumi.  (Global Architecture, no. 26.)  Tokyo:
A.D.A. Edita, 1973.

---

EERO SAARINEN; SKIDMORE, OWINGS & MERRILL

---

274.   Vivian Beaumont Theater, Lincoln Center; New York, NY; 1965; interior remodeled, 1981-1982.  A highly flexible, mechanized
theater originally designed to serve as home for a repertory company; its huge (10,000 square feet) stage can be used in either
proscenium or open-apron form.  It is housed on lower levels of

the same building which contains the Lincoln Center Library and Museum of the Performing Arts. Collaborating designer for the theater: Jo Mielziner. Consultants: Ammann & Whitney (structural); Syska & Hennessy (mechanical). General contractor: Turner Construction Co. SEE: Progressive Architecture (vol. 46) November 1965, 189-194; Interiors (vol. 125) December 1965, 84-91; Progressive Architecture (vol. 47) April 1966, 176-183 (for the Performing Arts Library and Museum).

---

## EERO SAARINEN; SMITH, HINCHMAN & GRYLLS

---

275. General Motors Technical Center; Warren, MI; 1956. Situated on a square mile of lightly wooded countryside, this extraordinary assemblage of 20 buildings plus a sizable man-made lake complete with fountains and a handsomely modeled stainless steel sheathed water tower has been called "a coordinated research town" and "an industrial Versailles." Particularly noteworthy is the use of walls and panels of vivid colors as enlivening accents inside and out. Engineers: Smith, Hinchman & Grylls. Landscape architect: Thomas D. Church; associate landscape architect: Edward A. Eichstedt. General contractor: Bryant & Detwiler Co. HONORS: AIA Honor Award, 1953; AIA Honor Award, 1955, for Central Restaurant Building; AIA Bicentennial List, 3 nominations. SEE: Architectural Forum (vol. 101) November 1954, 100-119. Architectural Forum (vol. 104) May 1956, 122-129.

---

## SAARINEN, SAARINEN

Eliel Saarinen won the AIA Gold Medal in 1947 and the Royal Gold Medal in 1950; in 1962 his son, Eero Saarinen, also won the AIA Gold Medal.

---

276. Christ Church; Minneapolis, MN; 1948/1949. Spare yet not severe, asymmetrical in plan yet serenely proportioned and balanced, here is a modest brick Lutheran church of lasting architectural value. In its sanctuary, natural light from a tall window masked from the congregation floods the altar. One long wall includes splayed panels of open jointed brick which add texture while they help absorb sound. Structural, acoustical and mechanical elements are "integrated into the form with no compromise." Associate architects: Hills, Gilbertson & Hayes. Acoustics: Bolt, Beranek & Newman. General contractor: Kraus-Anderson Inc. HONORS: AIA Bicentennial List, 1 nomination; AIA 25 Year Award, 1977. SEE: Architectural Forum (vol. 93) July 1950, 80-85. AIA Journal (vol. 66) May 1977, 28-29.

## SAARINEN, SWANSON & SAARINEN

277. Opera Shed, Berkshire Music Center; Stockbridge, MA; 1947. This concert hall for audiences of up to 1200, constructed inexpensively, primarily of wood, owes its fine acoustics to the loving care and attention to detail with which it was built. Its most striking structural feature is a series of laminated arches exposed above its roof; these arches link with supporting trusses. Acoustical consultant: Charles C. Potwin. SEE: Progressive Architecture (vol. 28) March 1947, 53-58. Architectural Review (vol. 101) May 1947, 163-164.

## JOSEPH SALERNO

278. United Church House of Worship; Rowayton, CT; 1962. A small church with an extraordinary roof that spirals skyward like an up-ended mollusk shell. Douglas fir was used to build a frame of intricately curved, laminated arch ribs which join in a spoked wheel at the back where the roof wraps around itself leaving room for a curved clerestory window. Structural engineer: Wayman C. Wing. HONORS: AIA Honor Award, 1963. SEE: Architectural Record (vol. 131) June 1962, 184-187.

## LOUIS SAUER ASSOCIATES

279. The Glass Palace, NewMarket; Philadelphia, PA; 1975. A prize-winner when originally designed as a commercial/retail/apartment complex to be known as Head House East, it was then enlarged, stripped of apartments, oficially dubbed NewMarket and popularly nicknamed The Glass Palace. Located in a neighborhood of 18th-and 19th-century townhouses, it presents a lively contrast: a collection of steel-framed, glass-walled cubes that face onto a "water plaza." Consultants: Design Associates (landscape); Joseph L. Hoffman & Assoc. (structural); M. Michael Garber & Assoc. (mechanical). HONORS: PA Design Citation, 1969. SEE: Progressive Architecture (vol. 57) April 1976, 76-79.

## SCHAFER, FLYNN, VAN DIJK

280.  Blossom Music Center; Peninsula, OH; 1968.  Acoustical considera-
      tions dictated this pavilion's unusual design in which a giant steel
      arch tilted 16 degrees from the horizontal serves as "backbone for
      an intricate lacework of wall and roof trusses."  Some 15,000 con-
      certgoers can be accommodated:  4500 within the pavilion, the rest
      on the sloping lawn around it.  Associate in charge of design:
      Ronald A. Straka.  Consulting architect:  Pietro Belluschi.  En-
      gineers:  R. M. Gensert Associates (structural); Byers, Urban,
      Klug & Pittenger (mechanical/electrical).  Acoustical consultants:
      Heinrich Keilholz, Christopher Jaffee.  General contractor:  Turner
      Construction Co.  HONORS:  AISC Architectural Award of Excel-
      lence, 1969.  SEE:  Architectural Record (vol. 145) June 1969,
      191-196.

## SCHIPPOREIT-HEINRICH ASSOCIATES

281.  Lake Point Tower; Chicago, IL; 1968.  This stunning instant land-
      mark, the first skyscraper ever entirely faced with undulating glass
      walls, when first completed was--with its 65 stories and 900 units--
      the tallest apartment house in the world.  Its design was suggested
      by sketches and models made in 1921 by Mies van der Rohe.  As-
      sociated architects:  Graham, Anderson, Probst & White.  Engi-
      neers:  William Schmidt & Assoc. (structural); William Goodman
      (mechanical/electrical).  Landscape architect:  Alfred Caldwell.
      General contractor:  Crane Construction Co.  HONORS:  AIA
      Honor Award, 1970; AIA Bicentennial List, 1 nomination.  SEE:
      Architectural Record (vol. 146) October 1969, 123-130 and cover.
      AIA Journal (vol. 53) June 1970, 80.

## SERT, JACKSON
Winner of the AIA's Architectural Firm Award, 1977

282.  Holyoke Center, Harvard University; Cambridge, MA; 1966.  One
      block square, this megastructure has many wings of varying heights,
      a 22-foot high arcade running through its center, and offbeat fenes-
      tration: occupants can decide whether their windows are paned with
      clear glass or filled with translucent panels.  Shops and a bank
      take up most street level space; offices and a health center occupy

most of the remainder of the building's 360,000 square feet. Associate: J. Zalewski. Associate and job captain: P. Krueger. Landscape architects: Sasaki, Dawson, DeMay Associates. Engineers: Cleverson, Varney & Pike. Contractors: George A. Fuller Co. HONORS: AIA Bicentennial List, 2 nominations. SEE: Architectural Forum (vol. 126) January-February 1967, [64]-77.

283. Undergraduate Science Center and Chilled Water Plant, Harvard University; Cambridge, MA; 1973. This strongly rectilinear, multi-level megastructure, which takes up a full city block, contains almost 300,000 square feet devoted to labs, classrooms and administrative offices, four large lecture theaters, three libraries and a glass-enclosed cafe. Also included is a chilled water plant, which occupies another 58,000 square feet. Principals in charge: Paul H. Krueger, Joseph Zalewski. Engineers: Lev Zetlin Associates (structural); Syska & Hennessy (mechanical); Bolt, Beranek & Newman (acoustical). General contractor: Turner Construction Co. SEE: Architectural Record (vol. 155) March 1974, 111-[118] and cover.

SERT, JACKSON & GOURLEY

284. Francis Greenwood Peabody Terrace (Married Student Housing), Harvard University; Cambridge, MA; 1964 (Illus. 35). In this unusual development, one structural unit--three bays wide and three stories high with a stair in its central bay--is repeated and used in contrasting combinations to create a lively mix of low-, mid- and high-rise buildings with varied facades. Apartments range in size from efficiencies to three bedrooms, a total of 499 in all. Associate: Joseph Zalewski. Landscape architects: Sasaki, Walker & Assoc. Engineers: Nichols, Norton & Zaldastani (structural); Sidney J. Greenleaf & Associates (mechanical/electrical). General contractor: Vappi & Company. HONORS: AIA Honor Award, 1965; AIA Bicentennial List, 4 nominations. SEE: Progressive Architecture (vol. 45) December 1964, 122-[133]. Kenchiku Bunka (vol. 20) November 1965, [101]-108.

[Opposite:] 35. Francis Greenwood Peabody Terrace, Harvard University. Sert, Jackson & Gourley. Photo: © Phokion Karas.

SERT, JACKSON & GOURLEY; HOYLE, DORAN & BERRY

285. Additions to campus, Boston University; Boston, MA; 1965. Given a
sliver of riverfront for additions to an existing campus, the architects chose to build relatively high-rise buildings and so preserve
space for plazas and terraces. Tallest is the 19-story Law and
Education Tower which is connected by a bridge to the Pappas Law
Library; another new building is the Student Union. All have vigorous facades alive with rhythmically repeating yet varied projec-
tions. SEE: Architectural Record (vol. 135) May 1964, 161-192.
Architectural Forum (vol. 120) June 1964, 122-123. Architectural
Design (vol. 35) August 1965, 383-388.

SKIDMORE, OWINGS & MERRILL
    In 1957, Louis Skidmore won the AIA Gold Medal; in 1962, Skidmore,
Owings & Merrill won the AIA's Architectural Firm Award. See also entry
nos. 119, 274, and 372.

286. Air Force Academy Chapel; Colorado Springs, CO; 1963. Focal point
of a prize-winning campus is this spectacular and colorful building
which bears, like sleek yet spiky trappings, 100 tetrahedrons clad
with aluminum sheeting and rising to 17 spires. Inside are separate chapels for Catholics, Protestants, and Jews. Partner in
charge and designer: Walter A. Netsch, Jr. Acoustical consultant: Bolt, Beranek & Newman. General contractor: Robert E.
McKee, Inc. HONORS: R. S. Reynolds Memorial Award, 1964;
AIA Bicentennial List, 2 nominations (for whole campus). SEE:
Architectural Record (vol. 132) December 1962, 85-92. L'Architecture d'Aujourd'hui (vol. 34, no. 108) June-July 1963, 10-[16].

287. Albright-Knox Art Gallery Addition; Buffalo, NY; 1962. The original
museum, a fine example of neoclassic architecture, was designed
by Edward B. Green in 1905. The added wing, though contemporary in its simple lines, blends in with it artfully. Faced primarily with matching white marble, it comprises two long galleries
and a garden restaurant, which bound a central sculpture court,
plus a third large gallery topped by a contrasting black cube which
contains an auditorium. Partner in charge of design: Gordon
Bunshaft. Design assistant: Sherwood A. Smith. Consulting engineers: Paul Weidlinger (structural); Jaros, Baum & Bolles
(mechanical/electrical). General contractor: The John W. Cow-
per Co. HONORS: AIA Honor Award, 1963. SEE: Architectural
Forum (vol. 116) March 1962, [118]-[121]. AIA Journal (vol. 39)
May 1963, 32-33.

288. American Republic Insurance Company National Headquarters; Des Moines, IA; 1965. This unusual eight-story office building with an inviting entrance court topped by a glassed-in terrace floor with dining and lounge facilities has been called "a load-bearing Lever House." A large and distinguished collection of modern art embellishes it throughout. Partner in charge: William S. Brown; partner in charge of design: Gordon Bunshaft. Engineering consultants: Paul Weidlinger (structural); Syska & Hennessy (mechanical). General contractor: Arthur H. Neumann & Brothers. HONORS: AIA Honor Award, 1967; AIA Bicentennial List, 1 nomination. SEE: Progressive Architecture (vol. 47) February 1966, 144-151. Skidmore, Owings & Merrill. Introduction and notes by Christopher Woodward. New York: Simon & Schuster, 1970. Pages 77-[82].

289. BMA Tower (Business Men's Assurance Company Building); Kansas City, MO; 1964. This 19-story office tower's gray glass window walls are recessed six feet back from a severely elegant white grid made of structural steel sheathed in gleaming marble. It is set in an expansive plaza paved in a distinctive purple brick which continues into the lobby area. Partner in charge: Bruce J. Graham. Engineers: Skidmore, Owings & Merrill (structural); Black & Veatch (mechanical/electrical). General contractor: Winn-Senter Construction Co. HONORS: AIA Honor Award, 1964; AISC Architectural Award of Excellence, 1964. SEE: Architectural Forum (vol. 121) July 1964, 86-[91].

290. Beinecke Rare Book and Manuscript Library, Yale University; New Haven, CT; 1963 (Illus. 36). In this stately treasure chest of a building, designed to house 800,000 volumes and over a million manuscripts, white marble is used in extraordinary fashion: in steel-framed slabs just 1 1/4 inches in thickness, thin enough to be translucent. During the day, light flows through the walls and accentuates the marble's veining; by night the library glows from within. Partner in charge of design: Gordon Bunshaft; partner in charge of coordination: David H. Hughes. Consultants: Paul Weidlinger (structural); Jaros, Baum & Bolles (mechanical). Contractor: George A. Fuller Co. HONORS: AIA Honor Award, 1967; AIA Bicentennial List, 1 nomination. SEE: Architectural Record (vol. 134) November 1963, 12-14. Progressive Architecture (vol. 45). February 1964, 130-133.

291. Carmel Valley Manor; Carmel Valley, CA; 1963. A retirement community of 170 residential units set on 23 acres of beautiful rolling country. Its gable-roofed, white stuccoed houses and casually landscaped grounds recall a Mediterranean village--comfortably "human scale." Landscape architects: Sasaki, Walker & Associates. General contractor: Williams & Burrows. HONORS: AIA Merit Award, 1964. SEE: Progressive Architecture (vol. 45) April 1964, 136-153. Architecture of Skidmore, Owings & Merrill, 1963-1973. Introduction by Arthur Drexler. New York: Architectural Book Publishing, 1974. Pages 264-267.

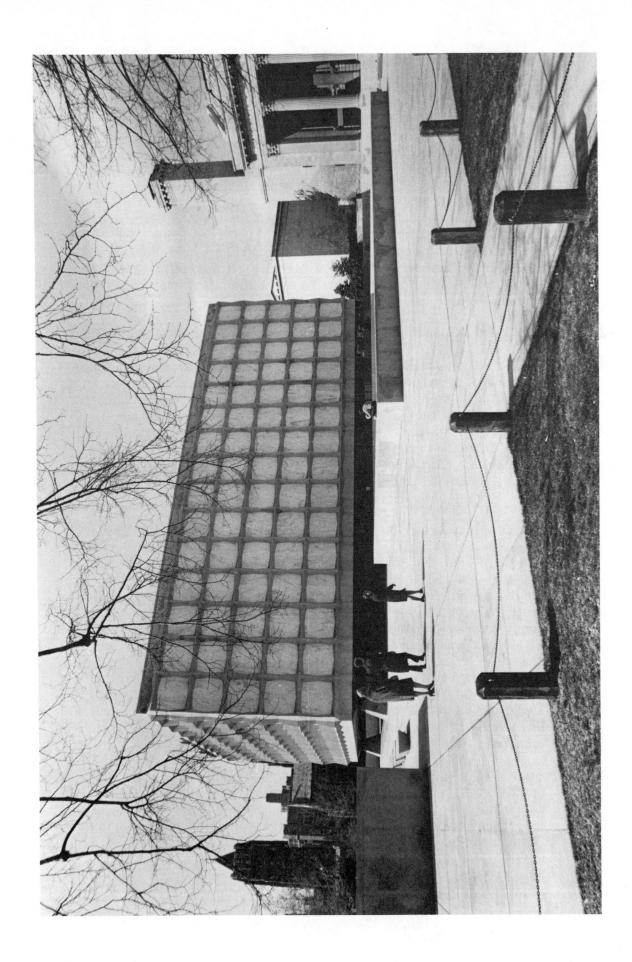

292. Central Facilities Building, Baxter Corporate Headquarters; Deerfield, IL; 1975. Focal point of a corporate complex set in a landscaped park is this building the roof of which is dramatically suspended by cables hung from two giant masts which rise 35 feet above the roof proper. The "central facilities" contained inside include a spectacular cafeteria--which among other things contains good-sized trees --an auditorium, a sales training center, and an executive dining room. Design partner: Bruce J. Graham; partner-in-charge: John K. Turley; senior architect: Brigitta Peterhans. Structural partner: Fazlur Khan. HONORS: AISC Architectural Award of Excellence, 1975. Chicago AIA Distinguished Building Award, 1976. SEE: Architectural Review (vol. 162) October 1977, 231-236. Architettura (vol. 23) December 1977, 442-447, 454-455.

293. Central Staff Office Building, Ford Motor Company; Dearborn, MI; 1957. Set on 90 landscaped acres, this huge and handsome administrative building designed to house some 3100 employees comprises about a million square feet of flexible office space plus parking for 2600 cars, a 500-seat conference room, a 625-seat cafeteria, lounges, a sandwich shop and an executive penthouse with private dining rooms and a roof garden. Most of its office space is contained in a 12-story structure 537 feet long. Partner in charge: J. Walter Severinghaus; project designer: Charles E. Hughes; project manager: Robert K. Posey. SEE: Architectural Record (vol. 121) March 1957, 242. Progressive Architecture (vol. 38) June 1957, 181-191.

294. Circle Campus, University of Illinois; Chicago, IL; 1965, phase 1. Unusual features of this urban campus on 106 acres include elevated walks, designed to serve as "pedestrian expressways," which come together at a central plaza that also serves as roof for a lecture center underneath. This elevated plaza has been called "one of the great spaces in college architectural planning." Partner in charge: Walter A. Netsch, Jr. Consultants: Sasaki, Dawson, DeMay Associates (landscape); Bolt, Beranek & Newman (acoustics). General contractor: Gust K. Newberg Construction Co. HONORS: AIA Bicentennial List, 1 nomination. SEE: Architectural Forum (vol. 123) September 1965, 21-45. Progressive Architecture (vol. 46) October 1965, 222-231.

295. Connecticut General Life Insurance Company; Bloomfield, CT; 1957. An insurance company's stylish low-rise office complex sited on 280 acres of amiable countryside. Glass walled, with few fixed partitions and with a main area which contains 400,000 square feet of floor space unbroken by structural columns, it boasts such amenities as a swan pond, Noguchi sculptures and elegant courtyards

[Opposite:] 36. Beinecke Rare Book and Manuscript Library, Yale University. Skidmore, Owings & Merrill. Photo: J. D. Levine; courtesy of Yale University.

and terraces. Engineers: Weiskopf & Pickworth (structural); Syska & Hennessy (mechanical/electrical). General contractor: Turner Construction Company. HONORS: PA Award Citation, 1955; AIA First Honor Award, 1958. SEE: Architectural Forum (vol. 107) September 1957, 112-127+. Architecture of Skidmore, Owings & Merrill, 1950-1962. Introduction by H. R. Hitchcock. New York: Praeger, 1963. Pages 62-73.

296. Headquarters building, Emhart Manufacturing Company; Bloomfield, CT; 1963. This strongly horizontal steel-and-concrete building caps a commanding suburban ridge. Its single story office portion --a modified hollow square--is raised on striking tree-like pillars above ground level; cars park beneath while, within the square, lab facilities are housed in a separate two-story structure. Partner in charge: Gordon Bunshaft; project manager: Allan Labie; design assistant: Natalie DeBlois. Engineers: Paul Weidlinger and Weiskopf & Pickworth (structural); Syska & Hennessy (mechanical). General contractor: George A. Fuller Co. HONORS: AIA Honor Award, 1964. SEE: Architectural Forum (vol. 119) July 1963, 88-[95]. Architecture of Skidmore, Owings & Merrill, 1963-1973. Intro. by Arthur Drexler. New York: Architectural Book Publishing, 1974. Pages 74-79.

297. Joseph H. Hirshhorn Museum and Sculpture Garden; Washington, DC; 1974. This controversial circular museum, designed during the uproar of the sixties, has been compared to both a doughnut and a military bunker. Raised on four 14-foot high piers above ground level, its facade is windowless except for one glazed horizontal slit. In its hollow center there's a circular courtyard, a fountain, and ample windows for its three stories of galleries. The sunken sculpture garden is reached by a tunnel under a nearby road. Partner in charge: Gordon Bunshaft. Consultants: Weidlinger Associates (structural); Jaros, Baum & Bolles (mechanical/electrical). General contractor: Piracci Construction Co. HONORS: AIA Bicentennial List, 1 nomination. SEE: Architectural Review (vol. 157) February 1975, 119-120. Artforum (vol. 13) February 1975, 56-62. Progressive Architecture (vol. 56) March 1975, 42-47 and cover.

298. Inland Steel Building; Chicago, IL; 1958. An unusual 19-story office building with all its structural columns outside its glass and steel curtain wall and its service core--elevators, air conditioning ducts, restrooms, stairs, etc.--confined to a windowless 25-story stainless steel tower set off at one corner of the total structure. General contractor: Turner Construction Co. HONORS: AIA Bicentennial List, 1 nomination. SEE: Architectural Record (vol. 123) April 1958, 169-178. Architecture of Skidmore, Owings & Merrill, 1950-1962. Intro. by H. R. Hitchcock. New York: Praeger, 1963. Pages 74-81.

299. John Hancock Building; New Orleans, LA; 1961. Windows are recessed behind a sunshading, precast-concrete frame in this tasteful

building which provides office space on the ground floor for the Hancock Insurance Company plus six stories of rental space above. It looks out on a raised, triangular plaza adorned by a sculpture fountain by Isamu Noguchi. Partner in charge: William S. Brown; partner in charge of design: Gordon Bunshaft. Associate architects: Nolan, Norman & Nolan. Engineers: Paul Weidlinger (structural); Syska & Hennessy (mechanical). General contractor: R. P. Farnsworth & Co. HONORS: AIA Merit Award, 1963. SEE: Progressive Architecture (vol. 44) September 1963, 126-135. Architecture of Skidmore, Owings & Merrill, 1950-1962. Intro. by H. R. Hitchcock. New York: Praeger, 1963. Pages 182-185.

300. John Hancock Center; Chicago, IL; 1970 (Illus. 37). This "blunt, black obelisk" is 1100 feet and 100 stories high. Geared for multiple uses, it contains 700 apartment units, over 800,000 square feet of office space and such amenities as restaurants, health clubs, a swimming pool and an ice skating rink. Partner in charge of design: Bruce Graham; associate partner in charge of design: Robert Diamant. Chief structural engineer: Fazlur Khan; project structural engineer: H. Srinivasa Iyengar. Structural consultants: Paul Weidlinger; Ammann & Whitney. General contractor: Tishman Construction Co. HONORS: AISC Architectural Award of Excellence, 1971; AIA Bicentennial List, 6 nominations. SEE: Architectural Forum (vol. 133) July/August 1970, 36-45. Architectural Review (vol. 151) April 1972, 202-210.

301. Lever House; New York, NY; 1952 (Illus. 38). A trendsetting triumph of an office building, this 24-story beauty faced with blue-green glass and stainless steel takes up just a fraction of its ample site; only its second story, supported on trim columns, describes an irregular hollow square over the bulk of its space. At ground level underneath are pedestrian walkways which hospitably invite passersby to enjoy the building's garden court. Partner for coordination: William S. Brown; partner for design: Gordon Bunshaft. Engineers: Weiskopf & Pickworth (structural); Jaros, Baum & Bolles (mechanical). General contractor: George A. Fuller Co. HONORS: AIA Honor Award, 1952; AIA Bicentennial List, 11 nominations. SEE: Architectural Forum (vol. 96) June 1952, 101-111. Architectural Record (vol. 111) June 1952, 130-135.

302. Manufacturers Trust Company Bank; New York, NY; 1954. A remarkable five-story bank on Fifth Avenue whose glass walls and glowing interior attract the passerby's attention to its prominently displayed giant vault, as artfully designed and finished as a piece of decorative sculpture. Partner for coordination: William S. Brown; partner for design: Gordon Bunshaft. Engineers: Weiskopf & Pickworth (structural); Syska & Hennessy (mechanical/ electrical). Interior consultant: Eleanor Le Maire. Builders: George A. Fuller Construction Co. HONORS: PA Award Citation, 1954; AIA Honor Award, 1954; AIA Bicentennial List, 1 nomination. SEE: Architectural Record (vol. 116) November 1954, 149-156. Architectural Forum (vol. 101) December 1954, 104-111.

37.   John Hancock Center--Chicago, Ill. (owner/developer).   Skidmore,
      Owings & Merrill.
      Photo:   courtesy of John Hancock Mutual Life Insurance Co.

38.　Lever House.　Skidmore, Owings & Merrill.
　　Photo:　courtesy of Lever Brothers Company

303. Marine Midland Building; New York, NY; 1968.  Here's a sleek, dark office tower, 52 stories high, built in the shape of a trapezoid to make most efficient use of its oddly shaped site and surrounded by a plaza which is enlivened by a vivid red, tipsy cube of a sculpture by Noguchi.  Partner in charge of design:  Gordon Bunshaft; partner in charge of administration:  Edward J. Matthews.  Engineers:  Office of James Ruderman (structural); Jaros, Baum & Bolles (mechanical).  General contractor:  Diesel Construction.  SEE:  Architectural Forum (vol. 128) April 1968, 36-[45].  Interiors (vol. 127) June 1968, 90-97.

304. Mauna Kea Beach Hotel; Kamuela, HI; 1965.  Tropical vegetation, painstakingly planted in a previously barren area, lends drama to this hotel's interior courtyards and reception areas and softens the tailored look of its neatly terraced facade.  Construction is of sand colored concrete set off by retaining walls of dark local lava.  Partner in charge:  John R. Weese; partner in charge of design:  Marc E. Goldstein.  Landscape architects:  Eckbo, Dean, Austin & Williams.  General contractor:  Haas & Haynie.  HONORS:  AIA Honor Award, 1967.  SEE:  Interiors (vol. 125) March 1966, 118-124.  Architectural Forum (vol. 124) May 1966, 80-87.

305. One Chase Manhattan Plaza; New York, NY; 1962.  Two city blocks were combined into one to permit this massive 60-story office building to be built straight up, without setbacks, while creating welcome open space around it in the crowded Wall Street area.  An executive lounge and dining room on the top floor enjoy spectacular harbor views.  Partner in charge:  J. Walter Severinghaus; partner in charge of design:  Gordon Bunshaft.  Consulting engineers:  Weiskopf & Pickworth (structural); Jaros, Baum & Bolles (mechanical).  General contractor:  Turner Construction Co.  SEE:  Architectural Record (vol. 130) July 1961, 141-150.  Interiors (vol. 120) September 1961, 112-117.

306. One Shell Plaza; Houston, TX; 1971.  When first completed, this 715-foot high, 50-story office tower set on a landscaped podium one block square was the tallest building west of the Mississippi.  Sheathed with 27 tons of travertine marble, it contains over 1,500,000 square feet of rentable space.  Partner in charge:  Bruce J. Graham.  Associate architects:  Wilson Morris Crain & Anderson.  Landscape architects:  Sasaki, Dawson & DeMay Associates.  Mechanical/electrical engineers:  Chenault & Brady.  General contractor:  Bellows Construction Co.  SEE:  Architectural Design (vol. 42) January 1972, 22-23.  Architectural Forum (vol. 136) April 1972, [24]-[39].

307. Pepsi-Cola World Headquarters; New York, NY; 1960 (Illus. 39).  A gleaming glass-and-aluminum 11-story office building which nestles with great self possession on a Park Avenue corner.  Generously set back from its legal building line and with its lobby areas further recessed, it boasts its own small plaza and sophisticated

39. Olivetti Building (Pepsi-Cola World Headquarters). Skidmore, Owings & Merrill.
Photo: © Ashod Kassabian 1981

detailing inside and out. Its name has recently been changed to the Olivetti Building. Partner in charge: Robert W. Cutler; project manager: Albert Kennerly. Engineers: Severud-Elstad-Krueger Associates (structural); Slocum & Fuller (mechanical/electrical). General contractor: George A. Fuller Co. HONORS: AIA Honor Award, 1961; Bard Award, 1964. SEE: Architectural Forum (vol. 112) March 1960, 102-108. Architectural Design (vol. 32) February 1962, 79-[82].

308. Portland Center; Portland, OR; 1968, first phase. In this delightfully "splashy" development, three rather severe apartment towers, several rows of townhouses, a shopping mall and related facilities share a midtown site with a spectacular fountain/plaza contoured in concrete to suggest a mountain setting alive with bubbling, rushing water. Partner in charge: David A. Pugh. General contractor: Portland Center Building Co. For parks and malls: landscape architects and urban designers: Lawrence Halprin & Assoc.; partner in charge: Satoru Nishita; resident landscape architect: David Thompson. Architectural consultants: Moore & Turnbull. Engineers: Gilbert, Forsberg, Deikman & Schmidt (structural); Yanow & Bauer (mechanical). General contractor: Shrader Construction Co. SEE: Architectural Forum (vol. 125) July-August 1966, 74-79. Bauen und Wohnen (vol. 21) April 1967, 134-137. Progressive Architecture (vol. 49) May 1968, 163-165. Process: Architecture (no. 4) February 1978, 159-184.

309. Rapid Transit Stations; Chicago, IL; 1971. In designing 17 stations--their boarding platforms, fare collection areas and areas in which to wait for connecting buses--the architects stressed exposed steel construction and painted the steel off-white throughout. Many station platforms have curved, glazed canopies which cantilever as much as 18 feet from both sides of a single row of columns. Partner in charge of design: Myron Goldsmith; project designer: Pao-Chi Chang. Coordinating engineers: DeLeuw Cather & Company. General contractors: J. M. Corbett Co.; Paschen Construction, Inc.; W. E. O'Neil Construction Co. HONORS: AISC Architectural Award of Excellence, 1971. SEE: Architectural Record (vol. 150) November 1971, 129-132.

310. The Republic; Columbus, IN; 1972. Home for a century-old daily newspaper, this is a long, low industrial building with considerable style in the Miesian tradition. Presses housed within are floated on a special pad to cut down noise and vibration; detailing is crisp and careful; and tempered glass walls put brightly painted equipment and architect-designed furnishings confidently on display. Partner in charge: Myron Goldsmith; project manager: George Hays; senior designer: Jin H. Kim; interior design: George Larson. Contractor: Dunlap Construction. HONORS: AIA Honor Award, 1975. SEE: Architectural Record (vol. 151) May 1972, 114-128. AIA Journal (vol. 63) May 1975, 26-43.

311.  Reynolds Metals Company General Office Building; Richmond, VA;
      1958.  A finely tooled corporate showplace set on 38 suburban
      acres and designed--from exterior column covers and sun louvers
      to ceilings and doorknobs--to display the many uses of aluminum.
      Its offices, dining facilities, reception areas and an auditorium oc-
      cupy a trim, low-rise building constructed in a hollow square
      around a formal, brick-paved courtyard.  Facilities planning/
      engineering/construction management: Ebasco Services, Inc.
      Acoustical consultants: Bolt, Beranek & Newman.  Landscape
      consultant: Charles F. Gillette.  General contractor: George A.
      Fuller Co.  SEE: Architectural Forum (vol. 109) September 1958,
      90-97.  Architecture of Skidmore, Owings & Merrill, 1950-1962.
      Intro. by H. R. Hitchcock.  New York: Praeger, 1963.  Pages
      82-89.

312.  Robert R. McMath Solar Telescope; Kitt Peak, AZ; 1962.  When built
      on its mountaintop site, this extraordinary structure--in effect "a
      camera with a 300-foot focal length"--was by far the largest solar
      telescope in the world.  It consists of a 500-foot long shaft, three-
      fifths underground, which is inclined 32 degrees to the horizontal
      and points to the north celestial pole.  The portion above ground is
      supported and stabilized by a 100-foot tall concrete tower.  Partner
      in charge: William E. Dunlap; senior designer: Myron Goldsmith.
      Chief structural engineer: Alfred Picardi; chief mechanical engi-
      neer: Sam Sachs.  Contractor: Western Knapp Engineering Co.
      HONORS: AISC Architectural Award of Excellence, 1963.  SEE:
      Architectural Forum (vol. 127) October 1967, [44]-[49].  Architec-
      ture of Skidmore, Owings & Merrill, 1963-1973.  Intro. by Arthur
      Drexler.  New York: Architectural Book Publishing, 1974.  Pages
      244-247.

313.  Sears Tower; Chicago, IL; 1974 (Illus. 40).  Tallest building in the
      world when completed, this 110-story office tower which tops out at
      1450 feet--the limit set by the Federal Aviation Administration for
      Chicago--is remarkable also for its innovative engineering.  Its
      structural strength in a notoriously windy city follows from con-
      struction as a cluster of "bundled structural tubes": nine inter-
      connected skyscrapers with ample cross bracing.  Partner in
      charge of design: Bruce Graham; chief structural engineer:
      Fazlur Khan.  Electrical and mechanical engineers: Jaros, Baum
      & Bolles.  Contractor: Diesel Construction.  HONORS: AISC
      Architectural Award of Excellence, 1975.  AIA Bicentennial List,
      3 nominations.  SEE: Architecture Plus (vol. 1) August 1973,
      [56]-59.  Architectural Forum (vol. 140) January/February 1974,
      24-31.

314.  Tenneco Building (formerly the Tennessee Building); Houston, TX;
      1963.  The glass walls of this handsome 33-story office tower are
      recessed five feet back from a structural framework which supplies
      shade against the Southwestern sun.  Its first two floors--very high

40.  Sears Tower.   Skidmore, Owings & Merrill.
     Photo:   courtesy of Sears, Roebuck and Co.

ceilinged and occupied by a bank--are set back still further from
massive exterior columns to create a 50-foot high entrance portico
and arcade. Consulting engineers: Bolt, Beranek & Newman
(acoustics); Engineers Testing Laboratory (foundation/materials);
Bramlett McClelland, Inc. (foundation design). General contractor:
W. S. Bellows Construction Corp. HONORS: AIA Honor Award,
1969; Bartlett Award, 1969; AIA Bicentennial List, 1 nomination.
SEE: Architectural Forum (vol. 119) September 1963, [124]-[131].
Architecture of Skidmore, Owings & Merrill, 1963-1973. Introduc-
tion by Arthur Drexler. New York: Architectural Book Publishing
Co., 1974. Pages 124-127.

315. 270 Park Avenue (formerly Union Carbide Building); New York, NY;
1960. Construction of this imposing, 52-story office tower, clad in
stainless steel, was complicated by the fact that three quarters of
its two-block site lay directly over two levels of heavily used railroad tracks! At street level it is surrounded by a generous amount
of open space and bisected by a 60-foot wide pedestrian arcade.
Partner in charge: William S. Brown; partner in charge of design:
Gordon Bunshaft; project designer: Natalie deBlois. Engineers:
Weiskopf & Pickworth (structural); Syska & Hennessy (mechanical/
electrical). General contractor: George A. Fuller Co. SEE:
Architectural Forum (vol. 113) November 1960, 114-121. Archi-
tecture of Skidmore, Owings & Merrill, 1950-1962. Intro. by H.
R. Hitchcock. New York: Praeger, 1963. Pages 142-151.

316. U. S. Naval Postgraduate School of Engineering; Monterey, CA; 1954.
An unpretentious yet attractive campus built on a budget. To cut
costs while providing labs and classroom buildings with sharp,
clean lines and tasteful detailing, prefabricated modular wood-and-
glass window wall units were used between framing concrete columns. Associate partner in charge of design: Walter A. Netsch.
Engineers: Isadore Thompson (structural); Keller & Gannon (mechanical). HONORS: AIA Merit Award, 1955. SEE: Architectural Record (vol. 115) June 1954, 150-157. Architectural Record
(vol. 117) April 1955, 159-171.

317. Wells Fargo Bank-American Trust Company branch bank; San Francisco, CA; 1959. Here's a dainty confection of a one-story bank:
circular, glass-walled, with a fanciful, wavy-edged roof that looks
from above like a pleated doily and is garnished at its center with
a blossom-shaped skylight. It's located on the plaza of SOM's
Crown Zellerbach building (see entry no. 119). General contractor:
Haas & Haynie. HONORS: AISC Award of Excellence, 1960. SEE:
Architectural Record (vol. 129) January 1961, 112-114. Japan Architect (vol. 36) April 1961, 70-72.

318. Weyerhaeuser Headquarters; Tacoma, WA; 1971. Hailed as "a building
that makes its own landscape," this immense corporate headquarters,
a quarter mile long, spans a valley and dams a natural creek into
a lake. Its five levels are intricately terraced and planted to wed

it visually with its woodland site. Landscape architect: Sasaki, Walker Associates. Landscaping contractor: Landscaping, Inc. General contractor: Swinerton & Walberg. HONORS: AIA Honor Award, 1972; Bartlett Award, 1972; AIA Bicentennial List, 2 nominations. SEE: Architectural Forum (vol. 136) March 1972, 20-27. Interiors (vol. 131) March 1972, 76-91.

319. Wyeth Laboratories, Inc. office and laboratory complex; Radnor, PA; 1956. Here laboratory, office and auxiliary facilities share 26 acres of rolling country. Sister low-rise buildings, connected by a glass-walled, one-story reception lobby and enclosing an appealing landscaped court, supply office space on one side, lab space on the other. Both are faced with blue-green glass and porcelain enameled panels of a deeper blue-green. Partner in charge: Robert W. Cutler; associate partner in charge of design: Roy O. Allen. Engineers: Seelye, Stevenson, Value & Knecht. General contractors: George A. Fuller Co. HONORS: PA Award Citation, 1954: AIA Merit Award, 1957. SEE: Architectural Record (vol. 121) April 1957, 195-200.

---

SKIDMORE, OWINGS & MERRILL; BROOKS, BARR, GRAEBER & WHITE

---

320. Lyndon Baines Johnson Library, University of Texas; Austin, TX; 1971. This monumental library--200 x 90 x 65 feet high with just a few narrow strips of windows and with an emphatically cantilevered top story--has vast, travertine-walled interior spaces and is set on a raised and formal plaza. Adjoining it is a long, low companion building which houses related collections and the LBJ School of Public Affairs. Partner for design: Gordon Bunshaft. Engineers: Paul Weidlinger-W. Clark Craig & Associates (structural); Gregorson, Gaynor & Sirmen, Inc. (mechanical/electrical). General contractor: T. C. Bateson Construction Co. SEE: Architectural Record (vol. 150) November 1971, 113-120. Architectural Design (vol. 43) February 1972, 87-90.

---

EBERLE M. SMITH ASSOCIATES

---

321. Greenfield Elementary School; Birmingham, MI; 1957. To make the most of a cramped, characterless site for two kindergartens and 18 classrooms to be grouped in threes, elementary classrooms in this long rectangular school face onto appealing courtyards and are divided into grade units by an imaginary line down the center. The two kindergarten rooms occupy a contrasting hexagonal building set

off to one side and reached by a covered walkway. HONORS: PA Design Award, 1957. SEE: Architectural Record (vol. 123) February 1958, 217-219. Progressive Architecture (vol. 41) March 1960, 131-137.

---

HAMILTON SMITH  see  MARCEL BREUER and HAMILTON SMITH

---

SMITH & WILLIAMS

---

322. Union Service Center, Local 887, UAW-CIO; Los Angeles, CA; 1957? Though largely glass-walled and located in a busy, distracting neighborhood, this inexpensively built, two-story center gains privacy and shade from "an architectural buffer zone" created by a strip of plantings alongside the building further enclosed by a long, enameled metal screen. Inside, structural elements--50-foot open web steel trusses on steel columns--are left exposed while stained glass insets brighten a stairwell. Landscape architect: Eckbo, Roystan & Williams. Engineers: Kolesoff & Kariotis (structural); J. F. Reardon (mechanical). General contractor: Roulac Company. HONORS: AIA Merit Award, 1958. SEE: AIA Journal (vol. 30) July 1958, 50-51. Arts and Architecture (vol. 76) May 1959, 16-17, 32.

---

SMITH, HINCHMAN & GRYLLS ASSOCIATES
See also entry no. 275.

---

323. First Federal Building; Detroit, MI; 1965 (Illus. 41). Located on a roughly triangular site, this 23-story office building has a tri-part structure with services consolidated in a central, windowless tower from which two glass-and-granite faced towers extend. The latter two towers are completely free of interior columns and together offer six corner office spaces per floor. This unusual design leaves space at ground level for a small plaza. Partner in charge: Bernard L. Miller; partner in charge of design: Sigmund F. Blum. General contractor: George A. Fuller Co. HONORS: AISC Architectural Award of Excellence, 1966; AIA Honor Award, 1967. SEE: Architectural Record (vol. 138) December 1965, 140-143. Thomas J. Holleman and James P. Gallagher, Smith, Hinchman & Grylls; 125 Years of Architecture & Engineering. Detroit: Wayne State University Press, 1978.

41.   First Federal Savings & Loan Building.   Smith, Hinchman & Grylls
Associates, Inc.   Architects/Engineers/Planners.
Photo:   Balthazar Korab

42.  Exodus House, East Harlem.  Smotrich & Platt.
Photo:  Norman McGrath

## SMOTRICH & PLATT

324.  Exodus House, East Harlem; New York, NY; 1969 (Illus. 42).  This
rehabilitation center for drug addicts is housed in a renovated five-
story tenement supplemented by a small concrete block structure
with strong, attractive lines that was built economically for the
program and is surrounded by hard-landscaped recreation areas.
Engineers:  William Atlas (structural); Wald & Zigas (mechanical).
General contractor:  Graphic Construction Co.  HONORS:  AIA

Honor Award, 1969; Bard Award 1969.  SEE:  Architectural Forum (vol. 129) October 1968, [62]-[65].

## PAOLI SOLERI

325.  Arcosanti; near Dugas, AZ; 1971-  .  A utopian community in the desert created by one of architecture's leading visionaries with the help of paying--not paid--apprentices.  Fanciful structures sandcast from concrete, rich with texture and color, replete with arcs, circles and other geometric motifs, and hung with bells made on the premises crowd together in a complex which one day, it is hoped, will house 3,000 people.  Included are foundries, studios and a crafts/visitors center.  SEE:  Progressive Architecture (vol. 54) April 1973, [76]-[81].  L'Architecture d'Aujourd'hui (no. 167) May-June 1973, [84]-[87].  Kenchiku Bunka (vol. 31) December 1976, 31-58.

## J. E. STANTON  see  WELTON BECKET and J. E. STANTON

## STEVENS & WILKINSON

326.  Georgia Center for Continuing Education, University of Georgia; Athens, GA; 1957.  This conference center contains such unusual facilities as its own closed-circuit TV station, an exhibit lounge, studio bedrooms and dining areas as well as meeting rooms and an auditorium.  A five-story red brick building with trim contemporary lines, it's built around a graciously landscaped courtyard.  Consulting architect: Louis Sarvis.  Landscape architects: Thomas D. Church & Assoc.; Edward L. Daugherty.  Structural engineers: Morris, Beohmig & Tindel.  General contractor: de Give, Dunham & O'Neill.  HONORS: PA Award Citation, 1955.  SEE: Architectural Forum (vol. 108) January 1958, 100-105.  Interiors (vol. 117) February 1958, 72-77.

## STICKNEY & HULL

327.  Los Gatos Civic Center; Los Gatos, CA; 1966.  Designed for a small

but growing community, here are what appear to be three separate, quietly handsome concrete-and-brick buildings--a library plus quarters for city administration and police--placed at the corners of a multi-level plaza. Under the plaza lies a council chamber which connects with all three surrounding structures thus linking the whole complex into a single building. Engineers: McClure & Messinger (structural); Chamberlain & Painter (mechanical/electrical). Landscape architects: Sasaki, Walker, Lackey Associates. General contractor: E. A. Hathaway & Co. HONORS: AIA Honor Award, 1967. SEE: Architectural Record (vol. 141) April 1967, 159-164. Lotus (vol. 5) 1968, [130]-[134].

---

## EDWARD DURELL STONE

---

328. Community Hospital of the Monterey Peninsula; Carmel, CA; 1962, expansion: 1972. A tastefully appointed hospital where all patients have private rooms and where there are attractive garden courts and balconies and a 72-foot square central courtyard with a pool and fountains. However, construction costs were not exorbitant. Resident architect: John C. Hill. Engineers: Pregnoff & Matheu (structural); G. M. Simonson (mechanical/electrical). Landscape architect: Georg Hoy. General contractor: Daniels & House. HONORS: AIA Merit Award, 1963. SEE: Architectural Forum (vol. 117) October 1962, [108]-[111]. Architectural Record (vol. 152) September 1972, 137-[144].

329. John F. Kennedy Center for the Performing Arts; Washington, DC; 1971 (Illus. 43). Planning for this building began in 1958 when Congress appropriated a 17-acre site on the banks of the Potomac for a national cultural center. Monumental and marble-clad, it is 100 feet high, 630 feet long and 300 feet wide and contains an opera house, a concert hall and a theater. Engineers: Severud-Perrone-Fisher-Sturn-Conlin-Bandel Associates (structural); Syska & Hennessy (mechanical/electrical). Stage consultant: Donald Oenslager. Acoustics: Cyril Harris. SEE: Theatre Design and Technology (no. 12) February 1968, [16]-27. AIA Journal (vol. 56) October 1971, 8. Interior Design (vol. 42) October 1971, 102.

330. Museo de Arte de Ponce; Ponce, PR; 1965 (Illus. 44). This museum, which makes the most of its tropical setting, comprises a small open-air theater, gardens and an expansive sculpture terrace as well as indoor exhibit space. On its second floor are a row of seven hexagonal galleries topped by skylights set into a space-frame structure of recessed triangles. Thanks to a system of open grilles, the galleries enjoy natural cross ventilation. Architect for construction supervision: Carlos Sanz. Engineers: Paul Weidlinger (structural); Cosentini Associates (mechanical/electrical).

43.   John F. Kennedy Center for the Performing Arts.   Edward Durell
Stone Associates P. C.


General contractor:  Edward J. Gerrits de Puerto Rico, Inc.
HONORS:  AIA Honor Award, 1967.  SEE:  Architectural Forum
(vol. 124) January-February 1966, 77.  Architectural Record (vol.
139) April 1966, [195]-206.

331.   Stuart Company plant and office building; Pasadena, CA; 1958.  Sited
on a downslope, this one- and two-story building and its adjacent
recreation area complete with pool are veiled from view by a 400-
foot long "Persian facade, " a lacy-looking grille made of openwork
concrete blocks.  Inside there's a dramatic atrium with a striking,
geometrically coffered ceiling and lush plantings.  Landscape architect:  Thomas D. Church & Assoc.  Engineers:  Hall, Pregnoff &
Matheu (structural); Stockly & Bamford (mechanical).  Contractors:
Myers Bros.; Brummet & Demblon.  HONORS:  AIA Honor Award,
1958.  SEE:  Architectural Forum (vol. 108) April 1958, 124-128.

44.  Museo de Arte de Ponce, Puerto Rico.  Edward Durell Stone Associates P. C.

---

EDWARD DURELL STONE; HARALSON & MOTT

---

332.  Fine Arts Center, University of Arkansas; Fayetteville, AR; 1951.
This peacefully rambling complex provides a unified environment
for a concert hall, a library and a three-story classroom block as
well as for indoor and outdoor theaters, workshops and exhibit
space.  Detailing and embellishment throughout are artful yet unpretentious and were designed by Stone--a native of Fayetteville--
to be built inexpensively.  Associate: Karl J. Holzinger, Jr.
Theater consultant: Edward Cole.  Landscape architect: Christopher Tunnard.  Sculptors: Alexander Calder; Gwen Lux.  General
contractor: Harmon Construction Co.  SEE: Architectural Forum

(vol. 95) September 1951, 164-169.  Arts & Architecture (vol. 68) November 1951, 35-37.  Architectural Review (vol. 112) September 1952, 156-159.  Progressive Architecture (vol. 33) September 1952, 126-127.

---

## HUGH STUBBINS

In 1967, Hugh Stubbins & Associates won the AIA's Architectural Firm Award.

---

333.  Citicorp Center; New York, NY; 1978 (Illus. 45).  Here's a towering office building that stands out not only because of its diagonal roof line--slanted as if for a solar collector but not yet bearing one-- but because of the popular appeal of The Market, its seven-story atrium entered at street level and designed for leisurely shopping, eating, and browsing.  Built on the site of an old church, Citicorp shares its space with that congregation's new quarters, also de- signed by Stubbins.  Project architect: W. Easley Hammer.  As- sociated architects: Emery Roth & Sons.  Consultants: LeMessurier Associates/SCI, Office of James Ruderman (structural and founda- tions); Joseph R. Loring & Assoc. (mechanical/electrical); Sasaki Associates (landscape).  Construction manager: HRH Construction Corporation.  HONORS: AISC Architectural Award of Excellence, 1978; Bard Award, 1978.  SEE: Building (vol. 234) May 5, 1978, 64-67.  Architectural Record (vol. 163) June 1978, [107]-116. Progressive Architecture (vol. 59) December 1978, 49-[69]. Process: Architecture (no. 10) 1979, 24-37.

334.  Francis A. Countway Library of Medicine, Harvard University Medi- cal School; Boston, MA; 1965.  This medical research center, shared by several institutions, provides temperature- and humidity- controlled quarters for up to 750,000 volumes and a variety of small, comfortable reading areas for scholars.  A bold and mas- sive square building with a large central court, it is six stories high with two more levels below ground and has reinforced con- crete framing and buff limestone walls.  Collaborator in design: Peter Woytuk; site planner: S. T. Lo.  Consulting engineers: LeMessurier Associates (structural); Greenleaf Associates (me- chanical).  General contractor: George A. Fuller Co.  HONORS: AIA Merit Award, 1966.  SEE: Progressive Architecture (vol. 46) November 1965, 166-177.  Arts and Architecture (vol. 83) April 1966, [20]-[23].  Process: Architecture (no. 10) 1979, 120-125.

335.  Loeb Drama Center, Harvard University; Cambridge, MA; 1960.  An early example of a theater designed for use in any of three modes: proscenium, arena, and in-the-round.  Housed in an elegant con- crete and brick structure ornamented with travertine and an intri- cate sunscreen, this highly flexible and mechanized auditorium can

45.  Citicorp. Center.  Hugh Stubbins and Associates, Inc. Architects.
Photo:  © Edward Jacoby

seat up to 600 people. Job captain: Gordon Anderson. Landscape consultant: John Wacker. Engineers: Goldberg, LeMessurier & Assoc. (structural); Delbrook Engineering (mechanical); Bolt, Beranek & Newman (acoustical). Theatrical consultant: George C. Izenour. Contractor: George A. Fuller Co. SEE: Architectural Record (vol. 128) September 1960, 151-160. Architectural Forum (vol. 113) October 1960, 90-97. Process: Architecture (no. 10) 1979, 130-135.

## HUGH STUBBINS; ASHLEY, MYER

336. Warren Gardens; Roxbury, MA; 1970. This 228-unit development, which makes the most of a hilly, rocky site, provides low-income housing in the form of attractive rowhouses many of which have entries on two different levels. Its construction--of clapboard and concrete block--fits comfortably into its New England setting. Engineers: Souza & True (structural); Samuel Lesburg Associates (mechanical). Landscape architect: John Lee Wacker. Contractor: Starrett Brothers & Eken. HONORS: AIA Design Award for Nonprofit-Sponsored Low and Moderate Income Housing. SEE: Architectural Record (vol. 149) Mid-May 1971, 86-87. House & Home (vol. 42) July 1972, [80]-[83]. Process: Architecture (no. 10) 1979, 92-105.

## WILLIAM B. TABLER

337. San Francisco Hilton Hotel; San Francisco, CA; 1964/1965. This 18-story, 1200-room downtown hotel includes seven layers of parking space enclosed within a rectangle of rooms and surmounted by an outdoor pool. Its windows are arranged in a checkerboard pattern to permit earthquake-resistant diagonal reinforcement of its poured concrete walls. Associate in charge: Eugene R. Branning. Engineers: Wayman C. Wing (structural); Jaros, Baum & Bolles (mechanical/electrical). General contractor: Cahill Brothers. SEE: Architectural Record (vol. 138) July 1965, [143]-150. Kenchiku Bunka (vol. 21) February 1966, [71]-77.

## TAC see THE ARCHITECTS COLLABORATIVE

TALIESIN ASSOCIATED ARCHITECTS see FRANK LLOYD WRIGHT; WILLIAM WESLEY PETERS and TALIESIN ASSOCIATED ARCHITECTS

PAUL THIRY, principal architect

338. Seattle World's Fair; Seattle, WA; 1962. An ingratiating world's fair located on 74 downtown acres and successfully designed to remain an asset to the city after its official close. High spots include Thiry's Coliseum; John Graham's Space Needle (q. v. ); Yamasaki's Federal Science Pavilion; the International Fountain, designed by Matsushita & Shimizu; and the main complex, designed by Naramore, Bain, Brady & Johanson. SEE: Architectural Forum (vol. 116) June 1962, 94-103. Architectural Record (vol. 131) June 1962, 141-148. Progressive Architecture (vol. 43) June 1962, 49-56+.

BENJAMIN THOMPSON

339. Design Research Building; Cambridge, MA; 1969. A retail store with a difference: a glittering, many-faceted showcase for home furnishings and clothes with added space upstairs for offices. Its glass walls float on concrete slabs that jut out at odd angles, cantilevered boldly from supporting concrete columns. Inside are many blunt yet stylish touches: clean-lined open staircases with black pipe railings; floors of brick, concrete or wood. Associate in charge: Thomas Green. Engineers: LeMessurier Associates (structural); Reardon & Turner (mechanical/electrical). Contractor: Canter Construction Co. HONORS: AIA Honor Award, 1971. SEE: Architectural Record (vol. 147) May 1970, 105-112. Interiors (vol. 129) May 1970, 108-[117]. Architectural Review (vol. 151) [28]-[34].

340. Mt. Anthony Union High School; Bennington, VT; 1967. This U-shaped, three-level, "inward looking" school has few windows on its outer margins; built around a courtyard, it has generously glazed corridors around the court's perimeter and most of its classrooms have windows that face onto those corridors. Exposed waffle slab construction adds interest to ceilings, colorful accent walls and vivid graphics further enliven the interior, and a spacious, skylit library is the school's central focus. Associate in charge: Thomas Green. Landscape architect: Carol R. Johnson. Engineers: LeMessurier Associates (structural); Shooshanian

Engineering Co. (mechanical). Contractor: George A. Fuller & Co. HONORS: PA Design Award, 1965; Award of Merit, Library Buildings Award Program, 1968. SEE: Architectural Record (vol. 143) January 1968, 120-[124]. Progressive Architecture (vol. 49) February 1968, 128-135.

## BENJAMIN THOMPSON, for THE ROUSE COMPANY

341. Faneuil Hall Marketplace and Quincy Market Restoration; Boston, MA; first phase: 1976, second phase: 1977. Here a once rundown but historic area has been transformed into a vibrant complex of restaurants and shops with office space inconspicuously provided upstairs in renovated landmarks. Well chosen graphics and hardy landscaping brighten pedestrian spaces; aisles alongside the complex's long buildings are glassed over to extend market space all year round. Principals: Benjamin Thompson, Thomas Green. Engineers: Zaldastani Associates (structural); J. C. Higgins Co. (mechanical). General contractor: George H. B. Macomber. HONORS: PA Design Citation, 1975; AIA Honor Award (Extended Use), 1978; Bartlett Award, 1978; AISC Architectural Award of Excellence, 1978; AIA Bicentennial List, 2 nominations. SEE: Architectural Record (vol. 162) December 1977, 116-127. AIA Journal (vol. 67) Mid-May 1978, 118-[143]. Interiors (vol. 138) January 1979, 66-71.

## THOMPSON, VENTULETT, STAINBACK

342. Omni International; Atlanta, GA; 1976 (Illus. 46). This spectacular steel, glass and limestone megastructure covers 5 1/2 acres and contains two office buildings, a hotel, an ice skating rink and an indoor family amusement center as well as many shops and restaurants. Flamboyant touches here include a 205-foot escalator that soars through a central Great Space, a laser beam sculpture, and 700 prisms positioned to split sunshine that comes through skylights into splashes of colored light. Associate in charge: Marvin Housworth. Consultants: Jimmy H. Kluttz & Assoc. (landscape); Lazenby & Assoc. (mechanical engineers); Prybylowski & Gravino (structural engineers); One + One (design). General contractor: Ira H. Hardin Co. HONORS: AISC Architectural Award of Excellence. SEE: Progressive Architecture (vol. 57) May 1976, 51-69. A + U: Architecture and Urbanism (no. 94) July 1978, 87-94.

46. Omni International. Thompson, Ventulett, Stainback, Inc.
    Photo: Bill Hedrich, Hedrich-Blessing

TIPPETTS-ABBETT-McCARTHY-STRATTON

343. Pan American World Airways Passenger Terminal, Kennedy International Airport; New York, NY; phase 1: 1960, phase 2: 1976. As originally built, this terminal was "revolutionary in style"; its oval, four-acre parasol of a roof was cantilevered from a glassed-in central core so planes could pull up under the roof for convenient boarding. When expansion became necessary, a much larger, fan-shaped terminal was added to it; together they accommodate today's larger planes and utilize a modified drive-to-the-gate system to load and unload passengers. Associate architects, phase 1: Ives, Turano & Gardner. Consulting architect, phase 2: Philip Ives. Contractors: Turner Construction Co. (phase 1); Corbetta, Humphreys & Harding (phase 2). HONORS: AISC Architectural Award of Excellence, 1961. SEE: Progressive Architecture (vol. 42) November 1961, 140-[145]. Architectural Record (vol. 160) October 1976, 125-140.

MAX URBAHN

344. Vehicle Assembly Building, John F. Kennedy Space Center; Cape Canaveral, FL; 1966. A colossus among buildings, this gigantic workshop is visible 14 miles away and contains 130 million cubic feet of space. Designed as a "garage" for space vehicles, its entry doors slide vertically to provide an opening 500 feet high and 70 feet wide. Engineers: Roberts & Schaefer Co. (structural); Seelye, Stevenson, Value & Knecht (mechanical/electrical/civil); Moran, Proctor, Mueser & Rutledge (foundation). HONORS: AIA Bicentennial List, 2 nominations. SEE: Architectural Forum (vol. 126) January-February 1967, 50-[59]. L'Architecture d'Aujourd'hui (no. 133) September 1967, [98]-103.

VENTURI & RAUCH

345. Dixwell Fire Station; New Haven, CT; 1974. Practicality, whimsy and sly references to the commonplaces of vernacular architecture coexist in this fire station with a difference. An almost square building set diagonally--for reasons of mobility--on its site, it is built of intensely red brick, is tidily detailed, and features a projecting banner of a wall which bears in giant letters the names of

local fire-fighting units. Engineers: The Keast and Hood Company (structural); Vinokur-Pace Engineering Services (mechanical/electrical). Contractor: J. H. Hogan. SEE: Architectural Record (vol. 159) June 1976, [111]-116. A + U: Architecture and Urbanism (vol. 78) January 1978, 3-80. Venturi and Rauch: The Public Buildings. (Architectural Monographs no. 1.) London: Academy Editions, 1978.

346. Guild House, Friends' Housing for the Elderly; Philadelphia, PA; 1963/1965. A six-story brick apartment house which contains 91 units designed for low-income elderly tenants. Its distinctive appearance stems from an oversized arched window above its entry and other facade details modeled after a Renaissance chateau at Anêt as well as from subtle variations of size in its other windows, in its bricks, and in the spacing of fence supports. Associated architects: Cope & Lippincott. Consultants: Keast & Hood (structural); Pennel & Wiltberger (mechanical/electrical). SEE: Progressive Architecture (vol. 48) May 1967, 124-148. Lotus (vol. 4) 1967/68, [98]-105. Venturi and Rauch: The Public Buildings. (Architectural Monographs no. 1.) London: Academy Editions, 1978.

WALLACE, McHARG, ROBERTS & TODD

347. Amelia Island Plantation; Amelia Island, FL; master plan: 1971, development (phase I) opened 1974. A resort/residence community of one-family homes and mid-rise apartment houses originally located in a series of "neighborhoods" on 450 acres and later doubled in size. Its sensitive design protects the area's animal and plant ecology--particularly its fragile oceanfront sand dunes-- from destructive incursions. HONORS: PA Design Award, 1973; Honor Award, ASLA Professional Competition, 1973. SEE: Landscape Architecture (vol. 63) April 1973, 239-250. House & Home (vol. 46) November 1974, 59-71. Urban Land Institute Project Reference File (vol. 10) October-December 1980, no. 16.

JOHN CARL WARNECKE
See also entry no. 29.

348. Asilomar Housing, Asilomar Beach State Park; near Monterey, CA; Phase I: 1959, gradually expanded thereafter. The original buildings at this conference center, located in a region of great natural beauty, were designed by Julia Morgan around 1920. The tasteful

and unassuming housing and lounge-conference facilities added by Warnecke are built of redwood, cedar and local stone; they maintain the site's serenity and harmonize well with the original buildings. Structural engineers: William B. Gilbert & Associates. HONORS: AIA Merit Award, 1960. SEE: Architectural Record (vol. 127) March 1960, 145-160. Architectural Record (vol. 140) August 1966, 123-138.

349. Hennepin County Government Center; Minneapolis, MN; 1976. This centerpiece to a new civic center was designed to combine "informality with monumentality." It comprises twin towers, 24 stories high--one intended for county offices, the other for district and municipal courts. Between the two towers is a 350-foot high glassed-in atrium boldly bordered by exposed steel diagonal bracing. Associated architects: Peterson, Clarke & Associates. Engineers: Ketchum, Konkel, Barrett, Nickel & Austin (structural); Donald Bentley & Associates (mechanical/electrical/plumbing). General contractor: Knutson Construction Company. HONORS: AISC Architectural Award of Excellence, 1977. SEE: Architectural Record (vol. 161) March 1977, 101-106.

## WARNECKE & WARNECKE

350. Residence halls, University of California; Berkeley, CA; 1959/1960. This attractive complex is appealingly landscaped with ample open space, including several sunken courtyards. It takes up almost all of three consecutive city blocks and combines eight reinforced concrete, nine-story dormitories, brightened on some facades by colored metal panels, with four two-story dining/recreation buildings with gracefully curving roofs. Exteriors of both kinds of buildings are enhanced by decorative cast stone grilles. Engineers: Isadore Thompson (structural); Dudley Deane & Associates (mechanical). Landscape architect: Lawrence Halprin. General contractor: Dinwiddie Construction Company. HONORS: PA Award Citation, 1959. SEE: Architectural Record (vol. 127) March 1960, 154-160.

## WARNER BURNS TOAN LUNDE

351. Hofstra University Library; Hempstead, Long Island, NY; 1967. An unusual, covered, pedestrian bridge which spans a turnpike assures accessibility for this concrete and glass library while calling attention to it. The two-story pavilion which contains the library's basic public services is surmounted by an eight-story tower.

Space is provided for a collection of 400,000 volumes. Partner in charge: Danforth W. Toan; associate/design: Yung Wang. Engineers: Severud, Perrone, Fischer, Sturm, Conlin & Bandel (structural); Stinard, Piccirillo & Brown (electrical/mechanical). Landscape architect: M. Paul Friedberg & Assoc. HONORS: Award of Merit, Library Buildings Award Program, 1968. SEE: Architectural Forum (vol. 126) January-February 1967, 78-79. Architectural Record (vol. 143) March 1968, 149-[164].

---

HARRY WEESE
   In 1978, Harry Weese & Associates won the AIA's Architectural Firm Award.

---

352. First Baptist Church and Chapel; Columbus, IN; 1965. A sternly geometric, brick church/school/chapel built around an enclosed court. Both church and chapel have steeply pitched roofs, covered in slate, while several exterior walls are rounded, recalling medieval architecture. Engineers: The Engineers Collaborative (structural); Samuel R. Lewis & Associates (mechanical). Landscape architect: Dan Kiley. General contractor: Repp & Mundt Construction Service. SEE: Architectural Record (vol. 138) December 1965, 113-[117]. Process: Architecture (no. 11) 1979, 32-35.

353. "Metro" subway stations; Washington, DC; first phase: 1977. Although built of simple materials--primarily concrete with touches of tile, granite and bronze--these have been called "the most noble series of underground halls and simple and elegant ground level stations." Grandly vaulted, coffered ceilings lend drama to the underground spaces. SEE: AIA Journal (vol. 64) December 1975, [38]-43. Architectural Review (vol. 163) February 1978, 99-102. Process: Architecture (no. 11) 1979, 134-139.

354. Milwaukee Center for the Performing Arts; Milwaukee, WI; 1969. Built on the banks of the Milwaukee River, this handsome travertine-sheathed center contains three auditoriums: a 2327-seat concert hall, a 526-seat theater with a thrust stage, and a multipurpose 482-seat recital hall. Acoustical elements in the concert space, Uihlein Hall, are not concealed; instead they have been "designed into the room." Theater consultants: George C. Izenour Associates. Acoustical consultants: Bolt, Beranek & Newman; Dr. Lothar Cremer. Engineers: The Engineers Collaborative (structural); S. R. Lewis & Associates (mechanical/electrical). Landscape architect: Office of Dan Kiley. Contractor: Klug & Smith Co. HONORS: AIA Honor Award, 1970; AISC Architectural Award of Excellence, 1970. SEE: Architectural Record (vol. 146) November 1969, 147-[164]. Process: Architecture (no. 11) 1979, 56-67.

355. William J. Campbell Courthouse Annex; Chicago, IL; 1975 (Illus. 47).
This wedge-shaped, 27-story jail on Chicago's Loop has a facade
that looks like an IBM card; its irregularly placed slit windows are
7 1/2 feet long but only 5 inches wide--the maximum width allowed
without bars by the Bureau of Prisons. Each prisoner has a private room and other amenities. Engineers: Severud-Perrone-
Sturm-Bandel (structural); H. S. Nachman & Associates (mechani-
cal/electrical). Landscape architects: Joe Karr & Associates.
General contractor: Turner Construction Co. HONORS: AIA
Honor Award, 1977; Chicago AIA 22nd Annual Distinguished Buildings Award. SEE: Inland Architect (vol. 19) July 1975, 7-13.
AIA Journal (vol. 66) May 1977, [28]-49.

## WHITTLESEY, CONKLIN & ROSSANT

356. Lake Anne Center; Reston, VA; 1966. This lakeside pedestrian plaza,
central to one of seven villages in a noted planned community, is
surrounded by low buildings, uniform in style, which contain shops,
cafes, offices and apartments. Even such details as its storefronts
and signs have been designed by architects. HONORS: AIA Bicentennial List, 1 nomination. SEE: Progressive Architecture (vol.
47) May 1966, [194]-[201]. G. E. Kidder Smith, A Pictorial History of Architecture in America. New York: American Heritage,
1976. Vol. I, pages 392-393.

## WOLF ASSOCIATES

357. Beatties Ford Road and Park Road branches, North Carolina National
Bank; Charlotte, NC; Beatties Ford Road branch: 1971; Park Road
branch: 1973. Both of these one-story, sleekly white branch banks
are strongly geometric in plan: Beatties Ford Road is triangular;
Park Road, a drive-in bank, is shaped like a parallelogram. Both
are designed for ready accessibility to the handicapped. Engineers:
Ray V. Wasdell Assoc. (structural); Mechanical Engineers, Inc.
(mechanical). HONORS: AIA Honor Awards, 1971 and 1974; Bartlett Awards, 1971 and 1974. SEE: AIA Journal (vol. 55) June
1971, 45-55. Architectural Record (vol. 153) June 1973, 111-120.
AIA Journal (vol. 61) May 1974, 41-49.

[Opposite:] 47. William J. Campbell Courthouse Annex. Harry Weese.
Photo: Hedrich-Blessing.

FRANK LLOYD WRIGHT
    Winner, Royal Gold Medal, 1941; AIA Gold Medal, 1949.

358.    Annunciation Greek Orthodox Church; Wauwatosa, WI; 1961.   An ex-
        traordinary and colorful church inspired by but not imitative of the
        Byzantine tradition.   Its shallow dome, about 100 feet in diameter,
        is covered with blue ceramic tile; lively patterns of arcs and cir-
        cles recur inside and out.   SEE:  Architectural Forum (vol. 115)
        December 1961, 82-87.   Ralph W. Hammett, Architecture in the
        United States.   New York:  Wiley, 1976.   Pages 225-227.

359.    China and gift shop for V. C. Morris, Maiden Lane; San Francisco,
        CA; 1949.   This remarkable store has no display windows; its
        blank facade of golden yellow brick is broken only by a fastidiously
        crafted, asymmetrical archway through which just a glimpse of the
        interior can be seen.   Light filters from above through a decorative
        screen that incorporates plastic disks and half bubbles; instead of
        stairs, there's a spiraling ramp that prefigures the more famous
        one in Wright's Guggenheim Museum (see entry no. 364).   SEE:
        Architectural Forum (vol. 92) February 1950, 79-85.

360.    Johnson Wax Company Research and Development Tower; Racine, WI;
        1950.   This innovative, 153-foot high research tower--when com-
        pleted, the tallest building ever erected without foundations under
        its side walls--was designed, said its architect, to provide "clear
        light and space all around every floor"; he called it "the Helio-
        lab. "   Its floors are cantilevered out from a central core; 40 feet
        square but with rounded corners, it is glazed with 2-inch wide
        glass tubing laid horizontally and sealed horizontally with plastic.
        Resident architect:  John Halama.   General contractor:  Wiltscheck
        & Nelson, Inc.   HONORS:  AIA Bicentennial List, 11 nominations.
        SEE:  Architect and Engineer (vol. 183) December 1950, 20-24.
        Architectural Forum (vol. 94) January 1951, 75-81.   Y. Futagawa,
        ed., Frank Lloyd Wright:  Johnson & Son Administrative Building
        and Research Tower....   Text by Arata Isozaki.   (Global Archi-
        tecture no. 1.)  Tokyo:  A. D. A. Edita, 1970.

361.    Kalita Humphreys Theater; Dallas, TX; 1959.   Housed in a contro-
        versial concrete building with oddly layered masses, this theater
        originally was designed to be used "in-the-round, " but to correct
        technical problems it was modified to create an apron stage arrange-
        ment.   A 32-foot section of its 40-foot circular stage revolves;
        many other facilities are highly mechanized.   Supervising architect:
        W. Kelly Oliver.   Lighting and mechanical consultant for stage:
        George G. Izenour.   Mechanical engineers:  Herman Blum Engi-
        neers.   Contractor:  Henry C. Beck Co.   SEE:  Architectural
        Forum (vol. 112) March 1960, 130-135.   Architectural Record
        (vol. 127) March 1960, 161-166.

362. Meetinghouse, First Unitarian Society; Madison, WI; 1951. The auditorium/chapel of this wood and stone building has a triangular, upthrusting roof that resembles a prow. Outside it forms a 40-foot spire; seen from inside, it frames a simple stone pulpit flanked by ample windows that open the room to views of trees and sky. Wright was a member of this congregation and his fellow parishioners, along with members of the Taliesin Fellowship. contributed labor to the construction of this meetinghouse. SEE: Perspecta (no. 1) Summer 1952, 16-17. Architectural Forum (vol. 97) December 1952, 85-92.

363. Price Tower; Bartlesville, OK; 1955. Both office space and apartments are contained in this 186-foot high reinforced concrete tower with gently angular lines and considerable cantilevering of its upper floors. Its facade is adorned by copper louvers and other copper facings, geometrically marked and preoxidized to a greenish cast. Mechanical engineer: Collins & Gould. General contractor: Haskell Culwell Construction Co. HONORS: AIA Bicentennial List, 1 nomination. SEE: Architectural Forum (vol. 104) February 1956, 106-113. Architectural Record (vol. 119) February 1956, 153-160.

364. Solomon R. Guggenheim Museum; New York, NY; 1959 (Illus. 48). A remarkable, often photographed art museum--New York's only permanent building by Wright--whose main gallery area is built in the form of one continuous, irregularly spiraling ramp around a great central well. Display walls slant outward, easel-fashion. HONORS: AIA Bicentennial List, 6 nominations. SEE: Architectural Record (vol. 123) May 1958, 182-190. Architectural Forum (vol. 111) December 1959, 86-93+. Y. Futagawa, ed., Frank Lloyd Wright: Solomon R. Guggenheim Museum.... Text by B. B. Pfeiffer. (Global Architecture, no. 36.) Tokyo: A.D.A. Edita, 1975.

365. Taliesin East; Spring Green, WI; 1959. Wright's own Eastern studio and home, sited on a hillside in the district of his "roots," begun in 1911 and repeatedly modified and enlarged over the years. Along with Taliesin West (see entry no. 366), it was workshop and home also to generations of architect-apprentices of the Taliesin Fellowship. (Taliesin is a Welsh word meaning "shining brow.") SEE: Architectural Forum (vol. 68) January 1938, 2-23. Architectural Forum (vol. 110) June 1959, [132]-[137]. Inland Architect (vol. 13) July 1969, 22-25. Y. Futagawa, ed., Frank Lloyd Wright: Taliesin East ... Taliesin West.... Text by Masami Tanigawa. (Global Architecture, no. 15.) Tokyo: A.D.A. Edita, 1972.

366. Taliesin West; near Scottsdale, AZ; 1959. Wright's desert studio and home, begun in 1934 and like Taliesin East (see entry no. 365) repeatedly enlarged and modified by the architect-apprentices of the Taliesin Fellowship working under Wright's supervision. HONORS: 25 Year Award, AIA, 1972. SEE: House Beautiful (vol. 83) December 1946, 186-195, 235. Architectural Forum (vol. 88) January

48.  Solomon R. Guggenheim Museum.  Frank Lloyd Wright.  Photo: Robert E. Mates; courtesy of the Solomon R. Guggenheim Museum, New York

8, 87-88.  House and Home (vol. 15) June 1959, 88-98.  Archi-
tural Forum (vol. 110) June 1959, 132-137.  Y. Futagawa, ed.,
nk Lloyd Wright: Taliesin East ... Taliesin West....  Text by
sami Tanigawa.  (Global Architecture, no. 15.) Tokyo: A. D. A.
ita, 1972.

OYD WRIGHT, until his death in 1959; WILLIAM WESLEY
S and TALIESIN ASSOCIATED ARCHITECTS thereafter

367.  Marin County Civic Center; San Rafael, CA; 1972.  An immensely
       long megastructure, richly and colorfully decorated, and roughly
       boomerang-shaped in plan.  It was designed to comprise 12 dif-
       ferent elements including an administration building, post office,
       and separate museums for natural history and art.  Its Hall of
       Justice alone boasts a 600-foot long gallery from which adjacent
       courtrooms look out on scenic bay and hillside views.  SEE: Ar-
       chitectural Forum (vol. 117) November 1962, 122-129.  Architec-
       tural Forum (vol. 133) December 1970, 54-59.  Y. Futagawa, ed.,
       Frank Lloyd Wright: Solomon R. Guggenheim Museum ... Marin
       County Civic Center.  Text by Bruce Brooks Pfeiffer.  (Global Ar-
       chitecture, no. 36.) Tokyo: A. D. A. Edita, 1975.

LLOYD WRIGHT
    The son of Frank Lloyd Wright.

368.  Wayfarers Chapel; Palos Verdes, CA; 1951.  Designed to be shel-
       tered by a grove of redwoods, this Protestant chapel which over-
       looks the Pacific has shoulder high walls of native stone topped by
       plantings and heavily bermed outside.  Above these low walls, on
       up through its arching roof, it is built almost entirely of glass
       sectioned off into geometric patterns by a framework of redwood.
       HONORS: AIA Bicentennial List, 2 nominations.  SEE: Architec-
       Tural Forum (vol. 95) August 1951, 153-155.  Arts and Architec-
       ture (vol. 83) October 1966, [22]-[26].

WURSTER, BERNARDI & EMMONS
    Winner of the AIA's Architectural Firm Award, 1965.  In 1969, Wil-
liam Wilson Wurster won the AIA Gold Medal.

369.  Center for Advanced Study in the Behavioral Sciences; Palo Alto, CA;

1954.  One-story redwood and glass buildings on a graciously land-scaped site provide quarters for scholars doing research on human behavior.  A cross-shaped central building houses administrative and group facilities; rows of separate study rooms, affording ample comfort and privacy, are located in long, narrow units distributed around the grounds.  Mechanical engineer: Buonaccorsi, Murray & Lewis.  Landscape architect: Thomas D. Church.  General contractor: Swinerton & Walberg.  HONORS: AIA Honor Award, 1956.  SEE: Architectural Forum (vol. 102) January 1955, 130-133.  Arts and Architecture (vol. 72) February 1955, 14-16.

370.  Ghirardelli Square; San Francisco, CA; 1965.  Quaint old red brick buildings, once occupied by a chocolate manufacturing firm, have been converted here into an enticing restaurant/shopping complex.  New buildings designed to blend in with the old and an underground garage for 300 cars have been added.  Structural engineer: Gilbert-Forsberg-Diekmann-Schmidt.  Landscape architect: Lawrence Halprin & Associates.  General contractor: Swinerton & Walberg Co.  HONORS: AIA Merit Award, 1966; AIA Bicentennial List, 3 nominations.  SEE: Interiors (vol. 125) October 1965, 98-109.  AIA Journal (vol. 46) July 1966, 46-47.  Process: Architecture (no. 4) February 1978, 103-118.

371.  Ice Houses I and II; San Francisco, CA; 1968.  An improbable but highly successful example of adaptive re-use: two staunchly hand-some brick warehouses, originally built in 1914 for cold storage, turned into wholesale showrooms for interior furnishings.  The architects made the most of original interior brick walls, high ceilings and wooden columns; they connected the two buildings at all upper levels with a boldly contrasting steel and glass "concourse tower" and added a plaza.  Engineers: G. F. D. S. Engineers (structural); G. L. Gendler & Associates (mechanical/electrical).  Landscape architect: Lawrence Halprin & Associates.  General contractor: Dillingham Construction Co.  HONORS: AISC Architectural Award of Excellence, 1969 (for concourse tower connecting the two renovated ice houses); AIA Honor Award, 1972.  SEE: Interiors (vol. 129) July 1970, 73, 84-85.  AIA Journal (vol. 57) May 1972, 40.

---

WURSTER, BERNARDI & EMMONS; SKIDMORE, OWINGS & MERRILL

---

372.  Bank of America World Headquarters; San Francisco, CA; 1969.  A 52-story office tower, faced with red granite and set on an appealing plaza, whose intriguing facade derives from San Francisco's traditional bay windows.  Above its plaza/lobby level, the building rises as a zigzag series of sawtooth bays unbroken except for contrasting detailing at the 15th and 37th floors and a series of irreg-

Engineers: H. J. Brunnier & Associates (structural); Skidmore, Owings & Merrill (mechanical/electrical). Landscape architect: Lawrence Halprin & Associates. Contractor: Dinwiddie-Fuller-Cahill (joint venture). HONORS: AISC Architectural Award of Excellence, 1970. SEE: Architectural Forum (vol. 131) October 1969, 70-71. Architectural Record (vol. 148) July 1970, 126-132.

# MINORU YAMASAKI

373. Michigan Consolidated Gas Company Headquarters; Detroit, MI; 1963. A precast concrete, 28-story office tower with surprisingly fanciful detailing in its 25-foot high lobby and in its soaring facade set with distinctive hexagonal windows. It is topped by an unusual "crown" designed to be illuminated at night. Associated architects and engineers: Smith, Hinchman & Grylls. General contractor: Bryant Detweiler Company. HONORS: AISC Architectural Award of Excellence, 1964. SEE: Architectural Forum (vol. 118) May 1963, [98]-[113]. Architectural Record (vol. 133) May 1963, [143]-150.

374. Reynolds Metals Sales Headquarters Building, Great Lakes Region; Detroit, MI; 1959. There's a light and airy feeling to this unusual suburban office building constructed around a skylit central well and almost completely surrounded by a reflecting pool. Two stories of offices supported on slim black columns hover above a recessed glass-enclosed entry floor and look out through a lacy sunscreen of gold-anodized aluminum. Design associates: Harold Tsuchiya and Gunnar Birkerts. Engineers: Ammann & Whitney (structural); Cass S. Wadowski (mechanical). Landscape architect: W. B. Ford Design Associates. General contractor: Darin & Armstrong. HONORS: AIA Honor Award, 1961. SEE: Architectural Record (vol. 126) November 1959, 161-168. Interiors (vol. 119) November 1959, 102-109. Architectural Record (vol. 136) September 1964, 169-184.

375. Temple and School Buildings, North Shore Congregation Israel; Glencoe, IL; 1964. Graceful aspiring lines that resemble plant forms characterize this religious complex built of reinforced and precast concrete. Light flows into the sanctuary through delicately wrought skylights and petal-shaped windows; harmonious expansion space for the sanctuary is provided innovatively by means of low platforms on either side of the main seating and an adjacent lobby/memorial hall. Resident architects: Friedman, Alschuler & Sincere. Project director: Henry J. Guthard. Engineers: Worthington, Skilling, Helle & Jackson (structural); Peter Turner (mechanical). Landscape architect: Lawrence Halprin. Contractor: Bolt, Beranek & Newman. SEE: Architectural Record (vol. 136) September

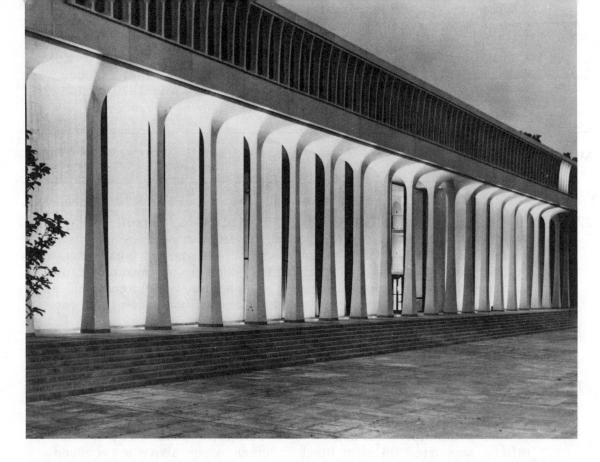

49. Woodrow Wilson School of Public and International Affairs, Princeton
University.
Photo: courtesy of Princeton University

1964, 176-177, 191-196. Architecture International (vol. 1) 1965,
96-103.

376. Woodrow Wilson School of Public and International Affairs, Princeton
University; Princeton, NJ; 1965 (Illus. 49). A colonnade of gracefully sculptured columns surrounds this oblong, high-ceilinged, two-
story building of "classic monumentality." It is set on a formal
podium within which is concealed a third level containing conference
and lecture halls; alongside lies a reflecting pool. Structural engineers: Worthington, Skilling, Helle & Jackson. Contractor: William L. Crow Construction Co. SEE: Architectural Record (vol.
134) December 1963, [103]-110. Architectural Record (vol. 138)
October 1965, 140-143.

## MINORU YAMASAKI; EMERY ROTH & SONS

377. World Trade Center; New York, NY; two tower buildings: 1971; expansion still in progress as of 1981. The twin towers of this gargantuan office complex briefly were, at 1350 feet, the tallest in the world. (Now superseded by the Sears Tower by Skidmore, Owings & Merrill, q. v. ) This complex also comprises four lower buildings set in a spacious plaza and an extensive system of underground concourses with numerous shops and restaurants and with connections to several subway lines. Engineers: Worthington, Skilling, Helle & Jackson (structural); Jaros, Baum & Bolles (mechanical). Main contractor: Tishman Realty & Construction Co. HONORS: AIA Bicentennial List, 1 nomination. SEE: Architectural Forum (vol. 134) May 1971, 7. Building (vol. 223) September 29, 1972, 43-47. Architectural Record (vol. 155) March 1974, 140-142.

## YAMASAKI, LEINWEBER

378. McGregor Memorial Conference Center, Wayne State University; Detroit, MI; 1958. On the east and west facades of this dignified campus center, two rows of marble-faced columns rise to neatly zigzagging concrete ceilings; its other two facades, blank at the sides, open at the center to a two-story high lobby topped with a skylight of gleaming diamond shapes and lined with columns and zigzag ceilings that echo those outside. Engineers: Ammann & Whitney. Landscape architect: Eichsted-Johnson Associates. General contractor: Darin & Armstrong, Inc. HONORS: AIA First Honor Award, 1959. SEE: Architectural Forum (vol. 109) August 1958, 78-83. AIA Journal (vol. 31) June 1959, 81.

## ZEIDLER PARTNERSHIP; BREGMAN & HAMANN

379. Toronto Eaton Centre; Toronto, Ontario, Canada; 1977, first phase. The centerpiece of this complex, located on a five-block site, is The Galleria, a shopping mall with scores of small shops; 860 feet long and 90 feet high, it is topped by an immense arching skylight. Also included in the complex are a major department store (Eaton's), high-rise office space and a parking garage. Coordinating partner: Sidney Bregman; design partner: Eberhard H. Zeidler. Engineers: C. D. Carruthers & Wallace Consultants Ltd.

(structural); H. H. Angus & Associates (mechanical/electrical). Construction management: The Foundation Co. of Canada Ltd. SEE: Architectural Review (vol. 163) February 1978, 103-108. Architectural Record (vol. 163) March 1978, 117-121. Process: Architecture (no. 5) 1978, 30-41.

HIGHLIGHTS

OF

RECENT

AMERICAN

ARCHITECTURE:

INDEXES

---

ADAPTIVE RE-USE  see  RESTORATION, RENOVATION AND ADAPTIVE
    RE-USE


AIRPORTS AND AIRPORT BUILDINGS

APARTMENT HOUSES  see  RESIDENTIAL DEVELOPMENTS


ARCHITECTS' STUDIOS

ARENAS  see  STADIUMS AND ARENAS

ART GALLERIES  see  MUSEUMS AND ART GALLERIES

ARTS CENTERS

Art Center College of Design; Pasadena, CA.  Craig Ellwood.  63
Carpenter Center for the Visual Arts, Harvard University; Cambridge, MA.
    Le Corbusier.  159
Center for Creative Studies, College of Art and Design; Detroit, MI.  Wil-
    liam Kessler.  150
Fine Arts Center, University of Arkansas; Fayetteville, AR.  Edward
    Durell Stone; Haralson & Mott.  332
John F. Kennedy Center for the Performing Arts; Washington, DC.  Ed-
    ward Durell Stone.  329
Mary Cooper Jewett Arts Center, Wellesley College; Wellesley, MA.  Paul
    Rudolph.  254
Milwaukee County War Memorial; Milwaukee, WI.  Eero Saarinen.  271
Paul Mellon Center for the Arts, Choate School and Rosemary Hall; Walling-
    ford, CT.  I. M. Pei.  219

BANKS

Beatties Ford Road and Park Road branches, North Carolina National Bank;
    Charlotte, NC.  Wolf Assoc.  357
Federal Reserve Bank of Minneapolis; Minneapolis, MN.  Gunnar Birkerts
    & Assoc.  30
First Federal Savings & Loan Association of Denver; Denver, CO.  William
    C. Muchow.  192
Manufacturers Trust Company Bank; New York, NY.  Skidmore, Owings &
    Merrill.  302
Park Central; Denver, CO.  Muchow Associates.  193
Seattle-First National Bank; Seattle, WA.  Naramore, Bain, Brady &
    Johanson.  202
Wells Fargo Bank-American Trust Co. branch bank; San Francisco, CA.
    Skidmore, Owings & Merrill.  317

BOTANICAL GARDENS  see  WINTER GARDENS

CHAPELS  see  RELIGIOUS BUILDINGS AND COMPLEXES

CHURCHES  see  RELIGIOUS BUILDINGS AND COMPLEXES

CITY HALLS AND CIVIC CENTERS  see  STATE CAPITOLS, CITY HALLS
    AND CIVIC CENTERS

CLUB HOUSES AND SOCIAL SERVICE CENTERS

COMMUNITY CENTERS

CONCERT HALLS & THEATERS
See also: ARTS CENTERS; STADIUMS AND SPORTS ARENAS

Milwaukee Center for the Performing Arts; Milwaukee, WI.  Harry Weese. 354

Mummers Theater; Oklahoma City, OK.  John M. Johansen.  125

New York State Theater, Lincoln Center; New York, NY.  Philip Johnson. 134

Opera Shed, Berkshire Music Center; Stockbridge, MA.  Saarinen, Swanson & Saarinen.  277

Robert S. Marx Theater, The Playhouse in the Park; Cincinnati, OH. Hardy Holzman Pfeiffer.  97

Tyrone Guthrie Theater; Minneapolis, MN.  Ralph Rapson.  235

Vivian Beaumont Theater, Lincoln Center; New York, NY.  Eero Saarinen; Skidmore, Owings & Merrill.  274


CONDOMINIUMS  see  RESIDENTIAL DEVELOPMENTS


CONFERENCE CENTERS AND STUDY FACILITIES FOR SCHOLARS
    See also:  RESEARCH AND TECHNICAL FACILITIES; CLUBHOUSES AND SOCIAL SERVICE CENTERS

Asilomar Housing, Asilomar Beach State Park; near Monterey, CA.  John Carl Warnecke.  348

Center for Advanced Study in the Behavioral Sciences; Palo Alto, CA. Wurster, Bernardi & Emmons.  369

Georgia Center for Continuing Education, University of Georgia; Athens, GA. Stevens & Wilkinson.  326

McGregor Memorial Conference Center, Wayne State University; Detroit, MI.  Yamasaki, Leinweber & Assoc.  378


CONVENTION CENTERS
    See also:  CONFERENCE CENTERS

Cobo Hall and Joe Louis Arena; Detroit, MI.  Giffels & Rossetti.  81

McCormick Place-On-The-Lake; Chicago, IL.  C. F. Murphy Assoc.  196

Renaissance Center; Detroit, MI.  John Portman.  232

Superdome; New Orleans, LA.  Curtis & Davis.  54

Veterans Memorial Coliseum; New Haven, CT.  Kevin Roche John Dinkeloo. 247


CORPORATE HEADQUARTERS  see  OFFICE BUILDINGS AND OFFICE COMPLEXES


COUNTY OFFICE COMPLEXES  see  STATE CAPITOLS, CITY HALLS AND CIVIC CENTERS


COURTHOUSES
    See also:  STATE CAPITOLS, CITY HALLS AND CIVIC CENTERS

Federal Center; Chicago, IL. Ludwig Mies van der Rohe. 178
Hennepin County Government Center; Minneapolis, MN. John Carl Warnecke.
349
Orange County Government Center; Goshen, NY. Paul Rudolph. 255
Richard J. Daley Center; Chicago, IL. C. F. Murphy Assoc. 198


ELEMENTARY SCHOOLS see SCHOOLS, ELEMENTARY AND SECONDARY


EXPOSITIONS see FAIRS AND EXPOSITIONS - BUILDINGS


FACTORIES see INDUSTRIAL BUILDINGS


FAIRS AND EXPOSITIONS - BUILDINGS

Expo '67 Theme Buildings, Man in the Community; Montreal, Quebec,
    Canada. Erickson/Massey. 65
Seattle World's Fair; Seattle, WA. Paul Thiry, principal architect. 338
Space Needle; Seattle, WA. John Graham & Co. 87
Tower of the Americas; San Antonio, TX. O'Neil Ford & Assoc. 70
U.S. Pavilion, Expo '67; Ile Ste. Hélène, Montreal, Quebec, Canada. R.
    Buckminster Fuller; Fuller & Sadao. 76


FIRE STATIONS

Dixwell Fire Station; New Haven, CT. Venturi & Rauch. 345


GARAGES

Temple Street Parking Garage; New Haven, CT. Paul Rudolph. 258
Vehicle Assembly Building, John F. Kennedy Space Center; Cape Canaveral,
    FL. Max Urbahn. 344


GOVERNMENT OFFICE COMPLEXES see OFFICE BUILDINGS AND OF-
    FICE COMPLEXES; STATE CAPITOLS, CITY HALLS AND CIVIC CEN-
    TERS


GREENHOUSES see WINTER GARDENS


GYMNASIUMS see SPORTS FACILITIES


HIGH SCHOOLS see SCHOOLS, ELEMENTARY AND SECONDARY

## HOSPITALS, SANITARIUMS AND MEDICAL CENTERS

## HOTELS AND MOTELS
See also: CONFERENCE CENTERS; MULTI-USE COMPLEXES

## HOUSING  see  RESIDENTIAL DEVELOPMENTS

## INDUSTRIAL BUILDINGS
See also: RESEARCH AND TECHNICAL FACILITIES

Stuart Co. plant and office building; Pasadena, CA.   Edward Durell Stone.
    331
Union Tank Car Repair Facility; Baton Rouge, LA.   R. Buckminster Fuller;
    Battey & Childs.   75
Vehicle Assembly Building, John F. Kennedy Space Center; Cape Canaveral,
    FL.   Max Urbahn.   344


JAILS  see  POLICE HEADQUARTERS AND JAILS


LABORATORIES  see  RESEARCH AND TECHNICAL FACILITIES


LIBRARIES

Auraria Learning Resources Center; Denver, CO.   C. F. Murphy Assoc.
    194
Bailey Library, Hendrix College; Conway, AR.   Philip Johnson.   128
Beinecke Rare Book and Manuscript Library, Yale University; New Haven,
    CT.   Skidmore, Owings & Merrill.   290
Boston Public Library Addition; Boston, MA.   Philip Johnson/John Burgee.
    137
Francis A. Countway Library of Medicine, Harvard U. Medical School;
    Boston, MA.   Hugh Stubbins & Assoc.   334
Hofstra University Library; Hempstead, Long Island, NY.   Warner Burns
    Toan Lunde.   351
James F. Lincoln Library, Lake Erie College; Painesville, OH.   Victor
    Christ-Janer.   47
Library, Tougaloo College; Tougaloo, MS.   Gunnar Birkerts.   33
Lyndon Baines Johnson Library, U. of Texas; Austin, TX.   Skidmore,
    Owings & Merrill; Brooks, Barr, Graeber & White.   320
Mount Angel Abbey Library, St. Benedict, OR.   Alvar Aalto.   2
New Orleans Public Library; New Orleans, LA.   Curtis & Davis.   53
Phillips Exeter Academy Library; Exeter, NH.   Louis I. Kahn.   146
Robert Hutchings Goddard Library, Clark University; Worcester, MA.
    John M. Johansen.   126
Sedgewick Library, University of British Columbia; Vancouver, British
    Columbia, Canada.   Rhone & Iredale.   240


MANUFACTURING PLANTS  see  INDUSTRIAL BUILDINGS


MARKETS  see  STORES, MARKETS, SHOPPING CENTERS AND SHOW-
    ROOMS


MEDICAL CENTERS  see  HOSPITALS, SANITARIUMS AND MEDICAL
    CENTERS

## MEMORIALS AND MONUMENTS

## MONUMENTS  see  MEMORIALS AND MONUMENTS


## MOTELS  see  HOTELS AND MOTELS


## MULTI-USE COMPLEXES

MUNICIPAL OFFICE COMPLEXES  see  OFFICE BUILDINGS AND OFFICE
  COMPLEXES; STATE CAPITOLS, CITY HALLS AND CIVIC CENTERS


MUSEUMS AND ART GALLERIES
  See also:  ARTS CENTERS

Albright-Knox Art Gallery Addition; Buffalo, NY.  Skidmore, Owings &
  Merrill.  287
Amon Carter Museum of Western Art; Fort Worth, TX.  Philip Johnson.
  127
Center for British Art and Studies, Yale University; New Haven, CT.
  Louis I. Kahn.  142
Corning Glass Center; Corning, NY.  Harrison, Abramovitz & Abbe.  107
Des Moines Art Center Addition; Des Moines, IA.  I. M. Pei.  211
East Building, National Gallery of Art; Washington, DC.  I. M. Pei.  212
Everson Museum of Art; Syracuse, NY.  I. M. Pei.  214
Herbert F. Johnson Museum of Art, Cornell University; Ithaca, NY.  I. M.
  Pei.  215
Hirshhorn Museum and Sculpture Garden; Washington, DC.  Skidmore,
  Owings & Merrill.  297
Kimbell Art Museum; Fort Worth, TX.  Louis I. Kahn.  145
Munson-Williams-Proctor Institute; Utica, NY.  Philip Johnson.  131
Museo del Arte de Ponce; Ponce, PR.  Edward Durell Stone.  330
Museum of Modern Art Additions and Sculpture Garden; New York, NY.
  Philip Johnson.  132
Museum Wing for Pre-Columbian Art, Dumbarton Oaks; Washington, DC.
  Philip Johnson.  133
National Air and Space Museum; Washington, DC.  Hellmuth, Obata &
  Kassabaum.  113
Oakland Museum; Oakland, CA.  Kevin Roche John Dinkeloo.  246
Sheldon Memorial Art Gallery, University of Nebraska; Lincoln, NE.
  Philip Johnson.  135
Solomon R. Guggenheim Museum; New York, NY.  Frank Lloyd Wright.
  364
University Art Museum, University of California; Berkeley, CA.  Mario
  Ciampi.  49
Walker Art Center; Minneapolis, MN.  Edward Larrabee Barnes.  19
Whitney Museum of American Art, New York, NY.  Marcel Breuer.  40
Yale University Art Gallery and Design Center; New Haven, CT.  Douglas
  Orr & Louis I. Kahn.  209


NEW TOWNS  see  PLANNED COMMUNITIES


OBSERVATORIES

Robert R. McMath Solar Telescope; Kitt Peak, AZ.  Skidmore, Owings &
  Merrill.  312

OFFICE BUILDINGS AND OFFICE COMPLEXES
See also: MULTI-USE COMPLEXES

## OPERA HOUSES  see  CONCERT HALLS AND THEATERS

## PIERS AND WATERFRONT COMPLEXES

## PLANETARIUMS

## PLANNED COMMUNITIES

## POLICE HEADQUARTERS AND JAILS

## POST OFFICES

Federal Center; Chicago, IL.  Ludwig Mies van der Rohe.  178

## RAPID TRANSIT STATIONS

"Metro" Subway Stations; Washington, DC.  Harry Weese.  353
Rapid transit stations; Chicago, IL.  Skidmore, Owings & Merrill.  309

## RECREATIONAL BUILDINGS AND COMPLEXES
See also: CLUBHOUSES; MULTI-USE COMPLEXES; PLANETARIUMS

Amphitheater and Plaza, Jacob Riis Houses; New York, NY.  Pomerance &
    Breines; M. Paul Friedberg.  229
Civic Auditorium Forecourt; Portland, OR.  Lawrence Halprin.  94
Climatron, Botanical Garden; St. Louis, MO.  Murphy & Mackey.  200
Corning Glass Center; Corning, NY.  Harrison, Abramovitz & Abbe.  107
Disneyland; Anaheim, CA.  Walt Disney.  60
Eagle Rock Playground Club House; Los Angeles, CA.  Richard J. Neutra.
    203
Expo '67 Theme Buildings, Man in the Community; Montreal, Quebec,
    Canada.  Erickson/Massey.  65
Faculty Club, University of California; Santa Barbara, CA.  MLTW/Moore
    Turnbull.  167
Florida's Silver Springs; Silver Springs, FL.  Victor A. Lundy.  164
Lila Acheson Wallace World of Birds Building, Bronx Zoo; New York, NY.
    Morris Ketchum, Jr.  151
Navy Pier Restoration; Chicago, IL.  Jerome R. Butler.  41
Omni International; Atlanta, GA.  Thompson, Ventulett, Stainback & Assoc.
    342
Portland Center fountain and mall; Portland, OR.  Lawrence Halprin.  308
Rainbow Center Mall and Winter Garden; Niagara Falls, NY.  Gruen Assoc.
    90
Sea Ranch Swim and Tennis; Sonoma County, CA.  MLTW/Moore Turnbull.
    169

## RELIGIOUS BUILDINGS AND COMPLEXES (CHAPELS, CHURCHES, SYNAGOGUES, ETC.)

Annunciation Greek Orthodox Church; Wauwatosa, WI.  Frank Lloyd Wright.
    358
Air Force Academy Chapel; Colorado Springs, CO.  Skidmore, Owings &
    Merrill.  286
Chapel of the Holy Cross; Sedona, AZ.  Anshen & Allen.  8
Chapel, Priory of St. Mary and St. Louis; near St. Louis, MO.  Hellmuth,
    Obata & Kassabaum.  111
Chapel, Tuskegee Institute; Tuskegee, AL.  Paul Rudolph; Fry & Welch.
    260
Christ Church; Minneapolis, MN.  Saarinen, Saarinen & Assoc.  276

RENOVATION  see  RESTORATION, RENOVATION AND ADAPTIVE RE-USE


RESEARCH AND TECHNICAL FACILITIES
    See also:  INDUSTRIAL BUILDINGS; UNIVERSITIES AND COLLEGES--
    BUILDINGS AND CAMPUSES

RESEARCH INSTITUTES  see  CONFERENCE CENTERS; RESEARCH AND TECHNICAL FACILITIES


RESIDENTIAL DEVELOPMENTS
    See also: MULTI-USE COMPLEXES.  For dormitories, see: UNIVERSITIES AND COLLEGES--BUILDINGS AND CAMPUSES

SHOPPING CENTERS AND SHOWROOMS see STORES, MARKETS, SHOPPING CENTERS AND SHOWROOMS


SOCIAL SERVICE CENTERS see CLUBHOUSES AND SOCIAL SERVICE CENTERS


SPORTS FACILITIES
See also: STADIUMS AND ARENAS

STADIUMS AND ARENAS
See also: SPORTS FACILITIES

## STATE CAPITOLS, CITY HALLS AND CIVIC CENTERS
See also:  POLICE HEADQUARTERS AND JAILS

## STATE OFFICE COMPLEXES see STATE CAPITOLS, CITY HALLS AND CIVIC CENTERS

## STORES, MARKETS, SHOPPING CENTERS AND SHOWROOMS
See also:  MULTI-USE COMPLEXES

Abramovitz. 104

University of Minnesota, East Bank Bookstore/Admissions and Records Facility; Minneapolis, MN. Myers & Bennett. 201

University of Nebraska, Sheldon Memorial Art Gallery; Lincoln, NE. Philip Johnson. 135

University of New Hampshire, Christensen Hall (dormitory); Durham, NH. Ulrich Franzen. 74

University of Pennsylvania; Philadelphia, PA.

Addition, Pender Laboratory, to Moore School of Electrical Engineering. Geddes, Brecher, Cunningham. 77

Alfred Newton Richards Medical Research Building. Louis I. Kahn. 141

University of Texas, Lyndon Baines Johnson Library; Austin, TX. Skidmore, Owings & Merrill; Brooks, Barr, Greaber & White. 320

University of Toronto, Scarborough College; Scarborough, Ontario, Canada. John Andrews. 7

Vassar College, Dormitory; Poughkeepsie, NY. Marcel Breuer. 36

Wayne State University, McGregor Memorial Conference Center; Detroit, MI. Yamasaki, Leinweber & Assoc. 378

Wellesley College, Mary Cooper Jewett Arts Center; Wellesley, MA. Paul Rudolph. 254

Western Washington State College, Ridgeway Men's Dormitories, Phase III, Bellingham, WA. Fred Bassetti. 21

Yale University; New Haven, CT.

Art Gallery and Design Center. Douglas Orr & Louis I. Kahn. 209

Beinecke Rare Book and Manuscript Library. Skidmore, Owings & Merrill. 290

Center for British Art and Studies. Louis I. Kahn. 142

David S. Ingalls Hockey Rink. Eero Saarinen. 265

Kline Science Center. Philip Johnson; Richard Foster. 140

Married Student Housing. Paul Rudolph. 253

Samuel F. B. Morse and Ezra Stiles Colleges. Eero Saarinen. 272

School of Art and Architecture. Paul Rudolph. 257


WATERFRONT COMPLEXES see PIERS AND WATERFRONT COMPLEXES


WINTER GARDENS

Climatron, Botanical Garden; St. Louis, MO. Murphy & Mackey. 200

Rainbow Center Mall and Winter Garden; Niagara Falls, NY. Gruen Assoc. 90


WORLD'S FAIRS see FAIRS AND EXPOSITIONS


ZOO BUILDINGS

Lila Acheson Wallace World of Birds Building, Bronx Zoo; New York, NY. Morris Ketchum, Jr. 151

# BUILDING NAME INDEX

# GEOGRAPHICAL INDEX

## CANADA

Burnaby, B.C.  Simon Fraser University.  Erickson/Massey.  66

Montreal, Que.
    Expo '67 Theme Buildings, Man in the Community.  Erickson/Massey.
        65
    Place Bonaventure.  Affleck, Desbarats, Dimakopoulos, Lebensold,
        Sise.  4
    U.S. Pavilion, Expo '67, Ile Ste. Hélène.  R. Buckminster Fuller/
        Fuller & Sadao.  76

Scarborough, Ont.  Scarborough College, U. of Toronto.  John Andrews.  7

Toronto, Ont.
    Toronto City Hall.  Viljo Revell; John B. Parkin Associates.  238
    Toronto Eaton Centre.  Zeidler Partnership; Bregman & Hamann.  379

Vancouver, B.C.  Sedgewick Library, U. of British Columbia.  Rhone &
    Iredale.  240

## PUERTO RICO

Cidra Municipality.  Housing for the Elderly.  Jorge del Rio & Eduardo
    Lopez.  59

Ponce.  Museo del Arte de Ponce.  Edward Durell Stone.  330

201

## UNITED STATES

### ALABAMA

Tuskegee.   Chapel, Tuskegee Institute.   Paul Rudolph; Fry & Welch.   260

### ARKANSAS

Conway.   Bailey Library, Hendrix College.   Philip Johnson.   128
Fayetteville.   Fine Arts Center, U. of Arkansas.   Edward Durell Stone.
   332

### ARIZONA

nr. Dugas.   Arcosanti.   Paoli Soleri.   325
Kitt Peak.   Robert R. McMath Solar Telescope.   Skidmore, Owings and
    Merrill.   312
nr. Scottsdale.   Taliesin West.   Frank Lloyd Wright.   366
Sedona.   Chapel of the Holy Cross.   Anshen & Allen.   8

### CALIFORNIA

Anaheim.   Disneyland.   Walt Disney.   60
Berkeley.
    Residence halls, U. of Calif. Warnecke & Warnecke.   350
    University Art Museum, U. of Calif.   Mario Ciampi.   49
    Wurster Hall, College of Environmental Design, U. of Calif.   Esherick,
      Olsen & DeMars.   69
Carmel.   Community Hospital of the Monterey Peninsula.   Edward Durell
    Stone.   328
Carmel Valley.   Carmel Valley Manor.   Skidmore, Owings & Merrill.   291
Chico.   Church of Our Divine Savior.   Quinn & Oda.   233
Concord.   Concord Pavilion.   Frank O. Gehry & Associates.   80
Daly City.
    Fernando Rivera Elementary School.   Mario Ciampi.   48
    Westmoor High School.   Mario Ciampi.   50
El Segundo.   Scientific Data Systems, Inc.   Craig Ellwood Assoc.   64
La Jolla.   Salk Institute for Biological Studies.   Louis I. Kahn.   147
Los Altos Hills.   Foothill College.   Ernest J. Kump; Masten & Hurd.   158
Los Angeles.
    CBS Television City.   Pereira & Luckman.   225
    Eagle Rock Playground Club House.   Richard J. Neutra.   203
    Los Angeles Bonaventure Hotel.   John Portman & Associates.   231
    Northwestern Mutual Fire Association Bldg.   Richard J. Neutra.   204
    Pacific Design Center.   Gruen Associates.   89
    Police Facilities Bldg., Civic Center.   Welton Becket & J. E. Stanton.
      25

CALIFORNIA (cont. )

## GEORGIA

Athens. Georgia Center for Continuing Education, U. of Georgia. Stevens & Wilkinson. 326
Atlanta.
    Hyatt Regency Hotel. Edwards & Portman. 62
    Omni International. Thompson, Ventulett, Stainback & Assoc. 342


## HAWAII

Honolulu. State Capital. Belt, Lemmon & Lo; John Carl Warnecke. 29
Kamuela. Mauna Kea Beach Hotel. Skidmore, Owings & Merrill. 304


## ILLINOIS

Carbondale. Faner Hall, Southern Illinois U. Geddes, Brecher, Qualls, Cunningham. 78
Chicago.
    Circle Campus, U. of Illinois. Skidmore, Owings & Merrill. 294
    860-880 Lake Shore Drive. Ludwig Mies van der Rohe. 181
    Federal Center. Ludwig Mies van der Rohe. 178
    Illinois Institute of Technology. Ludwig Mies van der Rohe. 179
    Inland Steel Building. Skidmore, Owings & Merrill. 298
    John Hancock Center. Skidmore, Owings & Merrill. 300
    Lake Point Tower. Schipporeit-Heinrich Associates. 281
    McCormick Place-On-The-Lake. C. F. Murphy Associates. 196
    Marina City. Bertrand Goldberg Associates. 84
    Navy Pier Restoration. Jerome R. Butler, Jr. 41
    O'Hare International Airport. C. F. Murphy Associates. 197
    Prentice Women's Hospital & Maternity Center, and Northwestern U. Downtown Campus. Bertrand Goldberg Assoc. 85
    Rapid Transit Stations. Skidmore, Owings & Merrill. 309
    Richard J. Daley Center. C. F. Murphy Associates. 198
    Sears Tower. Skidmore, Owings & Merrill. 313
    Water Tower Place. Loebl, Schlossman, Bennett & Dart; C. F. Murphy Assoc. 161
    William J. Campbell Courthouse Annex. Harry Weese & Assoc. 355
Deerfield. Central Facilities Building, Baxter Corporate Headquarters. Skidmore, Owings & Merrill. 292
Glencoe. Temple & School Buildings, North Shore Congregation Israel. Minoru Yamasaki. 375
Lisle. St. Procopius Abbey Church and Monastery. Loebl. Schlossman, Bennett & Dart. 160
Moline.
    Deere and Company Administrative Center. Eero Saarinen & Assoc. 266
    Deere West, John Deere and Company Administrative Center. Kevin Roche John Dinkeloo. 243
South Holland. Abraham Lincoln Oasis. David Haid. 93
Urbana. Illini Assembly Hall, U. of Illinois. Harrison & Abramovitz. 104

NEW YORK (cont.)

NORTH CAROLINA

NORTH CAROLINA (cont.)

Greensboro. Burlington Corporate Headquarters. Odell Associates. 208
Raleigh. Dorton Arena. Matthew Nowicki. 205


NORTH DAKOTA

Bismarck. Priory of the Annunciation. Marcel Breuer. 37


OHIO

Akron. Edwin J. Thomas Hall of Performing Arts, U. of Akron. Caudill
        Rowlett Scott; Dalton, Van Dijk, Johnson. 46
Cincinnati.
        The Cloisters. Hardy Holzman Pfeiffer Associates. 95
        Robert S. Marx Theater, the Playhouse in the Park. Hardy Holzman
            Pfeiffer Associates. 97
Painesville. James F. Lincoln Library, Lake Erie College. Victor Christ-
        Janer & Associates. 47
Peninsula. Blossom Music Center. Schafer, Flynn, Van Dijk & Assoc.
        280


OKLAHOMA

Bartlesville. Price Tower. Frank Lloyd Wright. 363
Edmond. Hopewell Baptist Church. Bruce Goff. 82
Oklahoma City. Mummers Theater. John M. Johansen. 125
Tulsa. 2300 Riverside Apartments. Harrell & Hamilton. 98


OREGON

Portland.
        Civic Auditorium Forecourt. Lawrence Halprin. 94
        Equitable Savings and Loan Building. Pietro Belluschi. 27
        Portland Center. Skidmore, Owings & Merrill. 308
St. Benedict. Mt. Angel Abbey Library. Alvar Aalto. 2


PENNSYLVANIA

Bryn Mawr. Eleanor Donnelly Erdman Hall, Bryn Mawr College. Louis
        I. Kahn. 143
Philadelphia.
        Addition, Pender Laboratory, to Moore School of Electrical Engineering,
            U. of Pennsylvania. Geddes, Brecher, Cunningham. 77
        Alfred Newton Richards Medical Research Building, U. of Pennsylvania.
            Louis I. Kahn. 141

TEXAS (cont.)

West Columbia. West Columbia Elementary School. Donald Barthelme &
Assoc. 20

VERMONT

Bennington. Mt. Anthony Union High School. Benjamin Thompson & Assoc.
340

VIRGINIA

Chantilly. Dulles International Airport Terminal Building. Eero Saarinen
& Associates. 267
Greenway. Science Bldg., The Madeira School. Arthur Cotton Moore/
Assoc. 188
Reston. Lake Anne Center. Whittlesey, Conklin & Rossant. 356
Richmond. Reynolds Metals Company General Office Bldg. Skidmore,
Owings & Merrill. 311

WASHINGTON

Bellingham. Ridgeway Men's Dormitories, Phase III, Western Washington
State College. Fred Bassetti & Co. 21
Seattle.
Seattle-First National Bank. Naramore, Bain, Brady & Johanson. 202
Seattle World's Fair. Paul Thiry, principal architect. 338
Space Needle. John Graham & Co. 87
nr. Seattle. Sea-Tac International Airport Expansion. Richardson Associ-
ates. 241
Tacoma. Weyerhaeuser Headquarters. Skidmore, Owings & Merrill. 318

WISCONSIN

Madison. Meetinghouse, First Unitarian Society. Frank Lloyd Wright.
362
Milwaukee.
Milwaukee Center for the Performing Arts. Harry Weese & Assoc.
354
Milwaukee County War Memorial. Eero Saarinen & Assoc. 271
Racine. Johnson Wax Company Research and Development Tower. Frank
Lloyd Wright. 360
Spring Green. Taliesin East. Frank Lloyd Wright. 365
Wauwatosa. Annunciation Greek Orthodox Church. Frank Lloyd Wright.
358

# INDEX OF DESIGN, ENGINEERING, AND CONSTRUCTION PROFESSIONALS AND FIRMS

If a firm name has varied in minor details--e. g., punctuation has changed or "& Partners" has replaced "& Associates"--all references to it are consolidated under one form of the name.